COMPANIONS IN CONTEMPLATION

What Columbia Seminary Colleagues and Friends Say

In *Companions in Contemplation*, Ben Johnson invites us to join him in the never-ending journey. He shares with us how he was invited into contemplation and the insights he has received along the way. And, he encourages us to let go of expectations and invites us to be fully alive to God in our own way.
-LAURA MENDENHALL, PRESIDENT

This book shares with the reader Ben Johnson's pathway into contemplation, while engaging and opening the secrets of many of the spiritual classics. Wisely, he does not provide a road map but signposts that point the way for anyone to explore the contemplative journey. I recommend this to those seeking a deeper spiritual life. -THOMAS G. LEWIS, DIRECTOR OF THE SPIRITUALITY PROGRAM

The movement into contemplation is an invitation into Mystery. When the interior landscape loses its familiar landmarks and former ways of knowing the Holy become confused, journeyers need a guide. *Companions in Contemplation* will be a trusted guide on an unknown way. -JULIE JOHNSON

Theologically sound and scholarly, *Companions in Contemplation* is a down to earth guide to a contemplative outlook. With freshness from his personal journey, Johnson eases the tension between seeking God and being found by God. The brief expositions, Biblical and Classical, crack open the door for our own contemplation. -DR. RON SMITH

This is Ben Johnson's best book to date. One loses all track of time as the rich experiences, metaphors and scripture passages lead into contemplation. This is a book to ponder over and over again as it prods our hunger for intimacy with God. Ben doesn't know all the answers, but he lives the questions.
-CHARLOTTE KELLER

Companions in Contemplation

Reflections on the Contemplative Path

Ben Campbell Johnson

Pathways Press

ACKNOWLEDGMENTS

Excerpts from *The Contemplative Heart* by James Finley, copyright © 2000 by Sorin Books, an imprint of Ave Maria Press Inc., PO Box 428, Notre Dame, Indiana 46556. Used with permission of the publisher. www.avemariapress.com

Excerpt from *New Seeds of Contemplation* by Thomas Merton, copyright © 1961 by The Abbey of Gethsemani, Inc. Reprinted by permission of New Directions Publishing Corp.

Excerpts from *Letters from the Desert* by Carlo Carretto, copyright © 1972 by Orbis Books, Maryknoll, New York 10545. Used with permission.

Excerpts from *Contemplative Prayer* by Thomas Merton, copyright © 1969 by The Merton Legacy Trust. Originally published as *The Climate of Monastic Prayer* by Cistercian Publications, Kalamazoo, Michigan, and reprinted by permission of Liturgical Press, licensor of Cistercian Publications.

Excerpts from *The Inner Experience* by Thomas Merton, copyright © 2003, published by HarperCollins Publishers, New York, New York.

ISBN: 1-4392-2014-X

Copies of this book may be ordered from:

www.Amazon.com
or
Pathways Press
P.O. Box 98213
Atlanta, Georgia, 30359

All scripture quotations are from the New Revised Standard Version
unless otherwise noted

Dedicated to:

My first reader: Kathleen O'Connor,
The Order of Manischewitz Retreat Group,
The Sunday Evening Contemplative Group that has walked
with me through these days:
Charlotte and James Keller, Lalor Cadley, Jane Hubbard,
Mary Ellen and Jeff Pendergrast, David Addis,
Sebring and Tom Lewis, Bill Cotterman, a friend, Julie Johnson,
and the members of a class, Beginners in Contemplation,
in July of 2007.

Contents

My Contemplative Prayer

O God, My Father,
     Take me by the hand,
     Lead me to the path,
     Place my feet in the way,
     And lead me into your presence.

As I wait before you,
     Cleanse the dross from my soul,
     Purify the thoughts and intentions of my heart,
     Enlighten my eyes that in your light I may see light,
     And, fill me with yourself that
          I may become an icon of your presence.

As I live in you and you live in me,
     May the false self die and the True Self arise;
     Let my self-shaped will dissolve
          Into your all-inclusive will
          Until I will one thing.
     Engulf my consciousness so that moment-
          by-moment I am united to you and
     Your kingdom comes,
     Your will is done,
     Your children receive daily bread,
          forgiveness of sin, and the guidance of
          your hand in their lives.

Preface

The gospels record Jesus' calling women and men to follow him. They were seized with such conviction that they left everything to follow his path. I believe that he calls us today to be his followers. This call not only forms us as his disciples, it persists, forever calling us deeper and deeper into God. It is a never-ending journey!

I wrote this book for several reasons. First, it gave me an opportunity to gather up the influences that have informed my journey. Writing also clarified my understanding of contemplation. I also wrote to invite other beginners like me to risk walking the dark path of contemplation. The title, *Companions in Contemplation*, is intentionally an invitation to my reader to walk into the strange life of "unknowing," "blindness," and "darkness," that characterizes this journey.

An overview of this book will mark the path I am inviting you to take. First of all, the book is divided into four major sections as the table of contents suggests. Each of these sections is connected by a theme, and together these sections focus on many important issues on the contemplative journey.

In the first section I set forth an understanding of my own journey, the ideas and experiences of my contemporaries, and the insights of those who have influenced me throughout my pilgrimage. The second section offers a report of my early experiences on this way. In my initial steps I wished for insights from others who had walked the way before me. I have endeavored to provide such. In the third section I set forth my meditations on a number of biblical texts that open up contemplative themes. The final section consists of meditations on some of the ideas that one of Merton's last books, *Contemplative Prayer*, inspired.

Read the first section for getting oriented to this way of prayer. Over a period of weeks, slowly work your way through the other sections. Short readings will help you get still and focused. If the ideas of this book do not speak to you, lay it aside and come back to it later.

Ben Campbell Johnson

Finding the Pathway

1

My Call to the Contemplative Path

The call, which came in my seventieth year, had the same ring of certitude and urgency as the call to follow Christ in my seventeenth year. It came unexpectedly at a time of great need and inner turmoil. Like other moments of call in my life, this most recent call came wrapped in simple words and events that became powerful directives. The unexpected happenings -- a voice, a vision, a chance meeting, a book purchased, and a startling statement -- combined to make clear to me a new direction of my life. In order for you to understand the profound importance of these events, I must tell you about my situation.

A State of Confusion

Just two years before these transformative occurrences, I had retired from Columbia Theological Seminary, where I had been a professor for twenty years. I should have anticipated the disturbance that retiring would have in my life, but I didn't. Before the date of my retirement, I thought several times about taking a full year off from work to make the transition into a different time structure. I ignored my intuition. Very shortly after my final day at the seminary, I began to deal with health issues. My blood pressure was out of control; I had a serious bladder infection; and, I began to accumulate fluid that landed me in the hospital with a diagnosis of congestive heart failure. These physical symptoms brought home to me the fact that I was entering into a new phase of life, one that could not continue as it had for the past twenty years. I canceled my entire schedule for the next year. It turned out that these physical challenges were only part of the aftermath of retirement.

For nearly fifty years I had lived with a passion to renew the church, and I recognized that I was beginning to lose that passion. I wondered if somehow I was being released from that struggle that had engaged me for five decades. In changes like this one, I think that we often wonder if the guidance is from God, and I knew that I could not fake a passion that I no longer possessed. So, in this changing situation I had to follow the guidance of the Spirit and embrace the new things that would be coming into my life. I knew that I was changing. I began to ask myself questions: What am I to make of this lack of drive to renew the church? Does it mean that this is not important to God? Does it mean that I should no longer devote my gifts and skills to this task? Does it mean that there is something else for me to do in these closing years of my life? Does it mean that I no longer have to bear the burden of the church?

Not only did I lose the passion to renew the church, I began to notice something that disturbed me even more, a loss of passion for God. I knew that I loved God, and yet I sometimes feared that my zeal to know and honor God had been driven by my vocation. Would my spiritual zeal completely fizzle when I was not teaching or preaching on a regular schedule? What God had given me in life, breath, insight, and memory were not to be ignored or to be put aside because I was no longer teaching at Columbia Seminary. Did my passion for God diminish along with my passion for renewing the church? Had there been some kind of spillover from my vocation into a feeling of loss in my relationship with God?

In the chaos that was gathering, I found myself questioning God: Do you want me both mentally and physically to become more relaxed and at ease? Do you want me to wait expectantly while my future is coming to me? Do you want me to learn how to live in the flow of life, not always pushing it? In a quiet, indiscernible way do you love me in this chaos in ways that I am neither able to notice nor to comprehend? In this questioning mode, I began to realize that God was strange and mysterious and wonderful, and at times so very perplexing!

I was not in a place to push the envelope, to step into some new venture, or to change other basic structures of my life. I found myself in a waiting mode. And, I knew from past experience that the heavenly schedule seldom matched my own. How do I wait? It was not the time for me to ask, "What next?" I was not yet to the "what next" phase. What would happen during the next year of my life? I seemed to know that I was in a posture of waiting, listening, and discerning the way of God in my life, and I was not nearly as distraught as I had been in similar situations earlier, but I did have symptoms of a person snatched from his safe and comfortable environment.

I began to experience a lack of focus. I had finished several books that were with the publisher. I had no new projects. I was restless, struggling in a kind of chaos that sometimes precedes a new creation. During this period I could not get my attention focused on a new project; I simply had no energy for writing or creating. This loss of focus and lack of energy left me with no clear sense of direction. I began to suffer from mild depression. My depression was more of an annoyance than a deep depression that made me dysfunctional. I had the taste of chaos in my mouth, but I was not afraid. I did not feel the floor moving beneath me dumping me into the abyss. I judged that I would not be in this place for the remainder of my life and that in some sense this upheaval was a normal part of the transition from my teaching career into whatever was next. The pathway of creativity seems always to pass through chaos; I was living between the "no longer" and the "not yet."

Not everything, however, was chaos in my life. An unexpected miracle happened and I do not know exactly when it occurred. I lost the dread and fear of dying. When I was nine years old or twenty-one years old or fifty years old, I had no idea that God would so completely erase from me the fear of dying and the coming eternity. The thought of eternity that once so stirred me no longer did. Even if there were nothing beyond this life, I still appreciated life, and I lived with the confidence that God was in the midst of life doing something that was beyond my understanding and imagination. Somehow it didn't seem to matter what God was doing or how God was doing it. I don't think often about dying, but when I do, I have positive images of what lies beyond.

I began to look at death as escaping from the womb of time and commencing the real adventure. This brief pilgrimage on earth has been merely preliminary for the great voyage into the unknown, into God, into an eternity of loving and worshipping and sharing in the everlasting becoming of God and of the whole of God's creation.

As my life unfolded after retirement, I sought to walk in faith and to believe that God had made a home in me, even though I could point to no evidence of it. I began to wonder about the deepening process: Is it true that, as I become my true self, the distance between God and me narrows? Does union with God mean becoming more congruent with my destiny? Does this congruence and union dissolve God's otherness and enable me to become ONE with God? Does this unity overcome the subject/object split? God is the I AM. Does God's I AM gather up my being into the divine being and move me toward fuller being?

I had a dream that seemed to symbolize the confusion that was going on in my life.

I am in a strange city (later I discover that it is New York). There are two ways to get to my destination. Instead of choosing the turn to the left that would take me down a lighted street, I choose to walk straight ahead. I am walking down that street mostly in the dark. I pass people on the street and occasionally I see shadowy figures in the darkness talking and gesturing. I have no idea who they are or what they are talking about, but I assume that they have noticed me as I pull my suitcase down the sidewalk. I am feeling anxious and uneasy in this neighborhood.

Soon, I am aware that I am near a metro line. I don't quite know how I got there and I notice that someone is now with me. I ask this person how to get to Marble Church, and this strange man who has joined me says this is the line to take to Marble. By some quirk I miss the regular entrance to the metro line. I find myself with this stranger standing six or eight feet below the track level. I have two bags and the stranger has one. We agree to help each other up the embankment along with our bags. I leave my bags and start to climb up the embankment so that I can board the train. The Stranger gives me a boost so that I can climb up the hill. He throws my bags up to me. I then turn to help him up the embankment. At this point the stranger disappears.

I make my way through the crowd standing and sitting on the train, and when I come to the front of the car, I notice on my left an old, weather-beaten man. He appears to be a street person with a red face, bleary eyes, stringy hair and large hands covered with a torn, worn-out pair of gloves. His posture attracts my attention as he slumps in a seat, where he stretches out and leans far back. I touch the old man and say something to him — something like bless you. He responds with, "Thank you, reverend." I am shocked that he realizes that I am a minister. And as if reading my thoughts, another voice cried out from the back of the car, "I knew you were a minister when you walked by." How, I wondered, did he know that I was a minister? He seemed to mumble something else to assure me that he recognized my vocation from my demeanor.

While I am thinking about this strange identification, I look toward the seat in front of the grungy street person; (the seat was turned backward so that the occupant was facing the old man). Instead of its being a person, the figure is Santa Claus all dressed but with no body. It was a one-piece Santa outfit, red trimmed in white. I notice but I do not have time to react to it.

I step beyond the seat of the old man and the Santa Claus suit. I am standing by another seat more like a bench than an individual seat. The bench extends around the edge of the car. I don't know whether it is filled with people or empty; it seems to me to be empty.

Suddenly, I feel something nip at my feet and ankles. Someone says there is an animal of some sort under the bench. I look down and I see a puddle that has spilled on the floor. The spill is mixed with broken glass and I cannot tell whether it is a drink or someone's vomit. I stooped to look under the bench and I saw a black dog with a short tail. He looked like a Schnauzer.

The phone rang. I awakened.

As I recalled the dream, I felt confused about its meaning. There were so many parts to the dream that seem disconnected, like the disconnects that I felt in my life. I went down a street I did not know; I pulled my baggage with me. I was frightened when I met persons I did not know in a place where I felt threatened. In the midst of my confusion and feeling of lostness I met a stranger. The stranger told me how to get where I was going. He helped me climb the hill, and he threw up my luggage. With that information I got on the train and was recognized, not by name, but by my profession. Still there is danger in a dog that will bite.

The dream depicts my existential situation – confused, lost, fearful, searching for a direction. It also confirms my identity – strangers recognize I am a servant of God. The alcoholic street person on the front seat and the voice from the rear of the coach both knew that I was a minister. I wonder if the stranger knew! And I wonder about the identity of the helpful stranger. I wonder if this stranger was a Christ figure.

What am I to make of this dream? If I had not written the dream and reflected on it, I would never, never have gotten any message. I think that it suggests to me that Christ comes to me in the form of a stranger; he enters into my confusion; and, he gives me help and guidance. Along my pathway, there are those who will recognize who I am and where I am going. There also will be messes to clean up, decisions about street people, empty Santa Claus suits, and dogs that bite.

As a sign that things were changing for me and that perhaps deliverance was on the way, I began to think about prayer. I began to question the various ways that I prayed and how I might pray differently. I asked, "How do I confess? Must I name my sins with the sound of my lips? Do I cry out for mercy and long for forgiveness? Or, is confession the simple acknowledgement of my humanness?" If I am before God, always before God, even my breath is confession, my being is confession, and just a moment's pause permits the flow of honest acknowledgement.

What is petition in the solitude of silence? Petition is nothing more than yearning, the longing that only the Spirit of God in me can express. The desire is too deep for words and only groans will suffice.

The First Mentor Retreat

For four or five years I had been thinking about inviting to a week of prayer eighteen or twenty friends that I had met in different parts of the country. First one reason and then another caused me to delay. Sometime in 2002, I spoke with a friend of mine about underwriting the cost of a gathering of lay and clergy for such a week. After thinking it over, he decided to underwrite the cost of the first retreat. The invitations went out and when the responses were in hand, twenty persons had expressed an interest in participating in the retreat.

In April of 2002, two weeks after Easter, we gathered at the Monastery of the Holy Spirit in Conyers, Georgia to live and pray with the monks. Most of us had had some experience in praying the Liturgy of the Hours (the seven stated times of prayer each day begun by Saint Benedict), but a few had not. By participating in this ancient liturgy, it seemed that the spirit of prayer surrounded all our conversations and groups during the week. My original urge to bring this group together sprang from my desire to help them know each other and experience the synergy that would inevitably occur. In the months before our first gathering, I thought about some of the spiritual exercises that had been meaningful to me – Lectio Divina, Group Spiritual Direction, and the Clearness Committee, to name a few of them. So in the time between the formal prayers, we had instruction and practice in these disciplines.

I had the desire for these friends, whom I knew and loved, to meet each other and to find significant connections that would nurture their lives and ministries. This dream was fulfilled beyond my expectations, but something occurred that I had not anticipated. I was changed more than anyone. And the change came to me in a manner completely unforeseen. I took to the retreat a life that was splintered, confused, and layered with depression. What happened to me that week changed my life!

The second night of the gathering, the subject of Group Spiritual Direction came up. I described to the group its dynamics. When I finished, one of the participants said, "Why can't we experience that this week?" I responded that there was no reason at all. So that evening I selected four persons who knew the exercise, and I asked them to meet at 6:00 a.m. for a review of the leader's role. I modeled for this group the experience of silence, sharing, listening for God together, and prayer. We divided the retreatants into four groups of five members each. The four persons that I had prepared led the experience, and I participated in one of the groups.

When it came my time to share in the group I said, "I have been retired for nearly two years, but I have not faced what that actually means. I would like to have discernment of what I am to do with the rest of my life." The leader invited the group to enter into silence and listen to what God might say to them regarding my need and request. As soon as I closed my eyes to enter into the silence, the Voice spoke to me in a question: "Do you really desire me?" I answered, "Mostly." Nothing memorable happened in the silence until just before the leader called time. In that instant I had an image appear in my mind (I think this is one meaning of vision in the Bible). I saw a person in a white robe with arms outstretched; I turned into those arms and felt the embrace. And, I heard in my deeper ear: "Ben, I love you; I really love you."

In a moment the time of silence ended and the leader asked what had come to me. I told the group about the words and the image that had powerfully gripped me. The group leader then asked others to share with me what had come to them. A couple said encouraging words and then Melanie said, "I saw you in a birth canal being born." Her response seemed to strike me deeper than that of others. Was I in the process of being born anew? After that small group experience the cloud over my spirit began to lift, the chaos began to be ordered, and I felt more hope than I had for a number of months. This encounter in the small group was the first formative event that happened to me during the week.

The second formative influence came to me on the last day of the retreat. We had experienced our closing and were ready to depart. I, and a number of other retreatants, stopped by the Monastery's bookstore. As I wandered among the shelves, I spotted a book by Thomas Merton, *Contemplative Prayer*; it was the last book that he wrote before his untimely death. I was strangely drawn to it, so I left the store with a copy of it in my bag. Something about this book fascinated me and I read it eagerly. I underlined thirty-nine sentences in the book that affected me – some inspired and informed me but others challenged me. Engaging this material was no "speed read," but rather a slow reflection on Merton's words and their meaning for me.

Since the beginning of the retreat, I had heard a voice and seen a vision, and Merton's book had powerfully drawn me. A third strange occurrence happened the week following the retreat. One day I stopped by the church to speak with our minister about a church matter. As I was entering his office, suddenly his door opened. He and Jeff, a church member, walked out of the office; under his arm Jeff had an album holding a half-dozen tapes. Spontaneously, he handed the album to me. I read the title, *Thomas Merton's Path to the Palace of Nowhere: The Essential Guide to the Contemplative Teachings of Thomas Merton*. It was written and recorded by James Finley, a man who had served for six years under the direction of Merton as a novice at the Abbey of Gethsemani in Kentucky.

Jeff asked, "Would you like to listen to these?"

What I actually felt inside was: "No, I hate listening to tapes." But, instead of these words coming from my lips, I heard myself saying, "Yes, I would." I took the tapes.

Thus the fourth indicator of change came in the form of a new outlook and a different set of feelings. For the previous two years. I had had difficulty seeing any purpose in my life – retired, career ended, a brief life before me, and likely illness and loss of health. I don't recall whether it was two or three days or two or three weeks, but I recall waking up to the fact that I no longer felt depressed. The dark cloud had lifted and disappeared. I began to see that I was entering into a new phase of life, one just as important as any other stage. Instead of big dreams and long-range goals, I realized that I needed smaller dreams and more immediate goals. In the midst of this transition, I began to recognize that engaging my life held great meaning for me. As a result of what happened to me at the retreat and during the weeks that followed, I felt a serious call to the contemplative pathway.

The final occurrence that belongs to this cluster of events happened the first day that I began listening to Finley's tapes on Merton. In spite of the fact that I felt no interest in listening to a dozen lectures by James Finley, I decided to put one of the cassettes into the player in my car. I was about halfway to my destination when I turned onto Scott Boulevard from Clairmont Road. As I was making the turn, I heard Finley saying:

"The word, God, is the metaphor for the infinity of the mystery the present moment manifests and, inversely, at one and the same time, the concrete immediacy of the present moment is realized to be the manifestation of the unmanifest mystery of God."[1]

I cannot explain why these words jarred me and gripped me so completely. I reversed the tape and listened to them again. Later, I replayed this definition of God and copied it on a sheet of paper. I memorized the words, awkward as they were. What did these words have to do with a contemplative life? I looked up every one of them in Webster's Unabridged Dictionary.

Rudolph Otto in his book, *The Idea of the Holy*, describes God as "something attractive and fascinating." Through these words the strange, seductive power of the holy got my attention, drew me into a dialogue with God, and caused me to wonder at the words that had so tightly grasped me. The words in this quote entered into me and I into them. Somehow I knew that they held enormous power for me; I knew they held a message that was destined to redirect my life.

This single, compound-complex statement seeks to balance opposites. The "present moment" acts as the fulcrum that balances "the manifestation of the mystery" on the one side and "the unmanifest mystery" on the other. I continued to reflect on the meaning of this statement: everything in the present moment from the air that I breathe, to the color of the sky, to the people and things that are flowing through my consciousness manifest God. God is not far away in some distant heaven looking down upon earth. Rather, God is here in the very stuff of

---

[1] From a set of tapes by James Finley on Merton's *Path to the Palace of Nowhere*.

everyday life. This Mystery is not confined to Sunday; it is not locked up in a book; and it is not under the control of the church or the theologians; no dogma controls it. This Mystery is contemporaneous with us; it is before us, beneath us, beyond us, within us, and coming to us every moment. These words were like a rich vein of ore or like diamonds hidden in the earth; they were strong, suggestive, and possessive; they were beckoning me to a new life.

Finley spoke of the present moment not only as manifesting the "infinity of the mystery," but he adds the inverse side, that the same moment manifests "the unmanifest Mystery" of life and being. If I could bring into my consciousness everything that is in me and in my world at this present moment, this awareness would not exhaust the depth of reality. Present also in this moment is the unmanifest mystery -- the mystery that I do not see, the perceptions that I do not possess, and the reality that is beyond my capacity to comprehend. The whole of Reality is present in the moment – the manifest and the unmanifest -- and my task in as complete a way as possible is to be mindful, to notice what is going on in me and in my world.

A month or so after being encountered and captivated by this statement, I showed it to a friend whose intelligence I deeply respect. I asked for his interpretation. He began at once to mark out the qualifying and descriptive words and in short order stated what was at the heart of the sentence. He was correct when he said, "God is the metaphor for both the manifest and the unmanifest mystery the present moment contains." But he did not include in his explanation why the mystery manifest in the present moment has such power to attract and invite. He did not explain to me what it would be like to engage this mystery in every moment. Neither did he document what living in the profound awareness of the present moment would be like. It is one thing to diagram a sentence, dissect the word's relationships, and state a clear meaning, and it is quite another venture to experience the reality to which this statement points. These words strain against their limits to express a Reality that defies simple reductionism.

What is a word? It is first a concept or an image that defines a thing or describes an action or amplifies more clearly the meaning of a thing or action. It is drawn both from the mental or material reality; it participates in that reality; but the word is merely a symbol. As a symbol the external or internal reality participates both in the mind and in the larger reality outside the human mind.

A word-symbol can be stored in memory. From memory the person can re-member it, and reuse the symbol in new logical operations. Through usage the original symbol goes through many transformations. Take the word GOD, for example. Its birth may have been in a thunderstorm, an earthquake or some other experience of awe, but the original breath of air that sounded "God," was not a completed symbol. The symbol, GOD, would be remembered and modified again and again through its connection with other experiences at other times and places.

I think that the birth of the symbol, GOD, arose from an event in which both the human and the holy participated. When the word was young and fresh, the repetition of the sound recalled the encounter with God, but in the process of time, the breath sound (word) got separated from the experience of the original stimulus that created it. Then the breath sound became a dead symbol in which neither holy nor human participated. Usage without experience emptied the symbol of its power.

And after 10,000 years of repetition and erosion, Finley seeks to restore again the ancient word to its original power and meaning. He fuses the material and the spiritual in a manner to save the symbol from pure spirit on the one hand and from dead materialism on the other. The word, GOD, must not be allowed to evaporate into the thin air of empty repetition, nor be identified with the original causation (wind, quaking or flood), but it must be held as a symbol.

When Finley says, "God," he makes reference to the eternal, enduring and inexhaustible nature of the mystery that surrounds us, the mystery that is our environment and the source of our fascination with life. How deep is the mystery in which we wade? How thick is it with unnamed pieces of reality? To this enchanted forest of impenetrable mystery the word "God" points.

But for Finley the present moment both offers and leads us into this mystery. The infinity of the mystery becomes evident or, at least, presents itself to us in the present moment. How long is a moment? It is an indefinite period of time, an instant, a second or a nanosecond. Perhaps it appears and departs before we are able to delineate when it began and when it ended. A moment may also be a point in time or a point in a series of events. It is now as opposed to then; it is *now*, not past; it is *now*, not future.

I consider the present moment as an invitation to see in a different way, to see every instant as a manifestation of the mystery. If I were able to do this, I would live on the point of being, at the edge of the new creation. Metaphorically, the present moment would become the vaginal canal that leads into the womb of God, the track through which time itself is born, moment-by-moment. But these explanations and metaphors mean nothing until we experience these fertile possibilities. The entrance to prayer has two doors – the manifest and the unmanifest.

Armed with a sense of call mediated to me through the words and vision, the book that I bought, the tapes that challenged and enlightened, the changes in my psyche, and the attention-grabbing sentence, I am discovering what it means to pray contemplatively. I am a novice on this pathway. I have read the classical literature; at least, I have looked at the page and pronounced the words. I have reflected on several of the classics, and sometimes I thought I understood their meaning. I feel called to walk this way. So I find myself on a pathway that I did not choose, guided by a hand that I cannot see, and led to a place that I do not know. For some strange reason I believe that this is the pathway I am to pursue, and I think the journey will be exciting. And I invite you, my reader, to become a companion with me on this journey.

2

The Hidden Pathway

Contemplation is an ancient, authentic, and vital way of prayer! Yet the pathway of contemplation seems to be hidden from many seeking souls. The prophets, the psalmists, and mystics from the Kabbalah tradition have practiced this ancient way of prayer. It is a way of prayer that was adopted by the desert fathers and mothers, installed in the monasteries of Saint Benedict, and practiced by the fourteenth-century mystics -- Teresa of Avila, St. John of the Cross, and the anonymous author of *The Cloud of Unknowing*. In more recent times, Father Thomas Keating of the Trappist monastery at Snowmass, Colorado, Father Thomas Merton of Gethsemane Monastery in Bardstown, Kentucky, and Father Tom Francis of the Monastery of the Holy Spirit in Conyers, Georgia have emphasized this practice. Though the people of God, both ancient and modern, have practiced this way of prayer, it still remains mysterious to most modern-day Christians. Yet, there are some bold, adventurous souls who have uncovered the entrance to this pathway and are making their way along its borders.

As a means of testing the understanding that today's church people have of contemplation, I chose a group from my circle of friends to ask a few basic questions. After selecting those whom I thought had some knowledge of contemplation, I asked them four questions:

1. What is your understanding of contemplative prayer?
2. How would you describe your experience of contemplative prayer?
3. What are the chief problems you have in praying contemplatively?

4. What are your expectations concerning contemplative prayer?

This chapter will be a compilation of the answers that each gave to these questions. I will indicate their ideas, experiences, problems and expectations with quotation marks.

Ideas of Contemplative Prayer

One of my respondents showed just how much he knew about contemplation by his opening remark: "He who speaks does not know; he who knows does not speak." He goes on to say, "As a beginner to contemplation, perhaps I might be forgiven for speaking about what I have simply tasted and know only in part. To me, contemplative prayer is a way to be still before God, open and receptive to God's love. 'Be still, and know that I am God' (Psalm 46:10). Contemplation is often experienced as a gift that emerges when one is completely present in the moment, open and alive. It does not result from straining to think holy or lofty thoughts. In fact, as soon as I begin to *think* about contemplation, to conceptualize it, the *experience* of contemplation fades. So, contemplation is a gift, an experience of knowing God. As the Psalmist urges us to 'be still,' there is a certain inner stillness that allows one to perceive and receive the gift of contemplation."

While Dan emphasizes stillness, Patricia focuses on the present moment. She states briefly but succinctly: "Contemplative Prayer is being totally present before God in the present moment. Contemplation calls me to empty my head of other thoughts, especially things I have to do, things I ought not to have done, and all the requests I customarily make in my prayers."

Ellen thinks of contemplative prayer as "an exercise in loving God. It means to become as a child and to lean into Abba's arms resting without words, reason, or anxiety. Just as a child drinks in the security of a parent's arms, so are we able to fold into God with only 'I love you' on our lips. Speech has no function: we remain still in our love for God and wait on God's Spirit to speak."

A Spiritual Director suggests, "Contemplative prayer is encountering God in the 'sacred center' of my being, in a space that is both nameless and timeless. In this place I can commune with God beyond words and beyond thoughts. At this center I can open myself, surrender myself to love God and to experience God's love." This description gets to the heart of the contemplative experience.

A friend, whom I providentially met far from my home, defines contemplation like this: "Contemplative prayer is a real relationship, real intimacy with God. I am beginning to think that whenever I am living as the person I was created to be, that is, not 'playing a role,' I am living contemplative prayer. Contemplation for me is not necessarily quiet or in solitude. I find it is essential to have silence and solitude, so that I have space for experiencing the goodness of God, but I agree with Gerald May who said that contemplation is diving into living and acting in the immediacy of life-as-it-is. Psychologists have spoken of something similar when they speak of 'peak moments' when life flows in ways that feel most alive, most creative, and most meaningful. This, for me, is contemplative prayer in daily life."

An associate with whom I worked many hours captured with words what contemplative prayer means: "Contemplative prayer is simply being fully alive and present to the Living God. There are no tricks, no gimmicks and no pretense. Like the old hymn says, 'Just as I am...' I enter into the great I AM. Many in the spiritual tradition think that contemplative prayer is a 'higher' form of prayer. I disagree. There are no levels in prayer...prayer is prayer and genuine prayer is always a gift from God. People who do not try so hard have an easier time with contemplative prayer -- children, simple people, the dying and the people who don't even know there is such a thing as 'contemplative prayer.' We cannot will ourselves into God's presence; we present ourselves to God and God graces us by sweeping us up into her/his holy heart. I am suspicious of people who strive after contemplative prayer. What is their motivation? I am cautious about teaching and about guiding people into contemplation until I notice God inviting them. After we sort through their motives, we can walk together along the contemplative pathway.

"All persons are unique and I do think that any of us can 'ready ourselves' for God. I like to use the example of the ways we get to sleep. Sometimes we simply fall asleep -- in class, on the train, or lying in a meadow on a spring afternoon. But generally, we prepare for bedtime. We may change our pace, our clothes, or our posture. We may read or listen to music or simply be still. In the end sleep comes as a gift and takes us away. The more we try to force ourselves to go to sleep, the more futile the task becomes. Worry, counting sheep, or tossing about only confounds our efforts. In the end, we become still and the gift of sleep comes to us. So too it is with prayer, especially contemplative prayer. Beyond our striving, beyond our images, beyond our words, and even beyond the beyond, the Holy One of the Beyond graces us, and we come to rest in Love.

"It can be dangerous to seek out this experience and over-indulge, even to become gluttonous. Remember how children get intensely involved; they cease and the balance of life returns. All is gift. Play time, work time, bath time, and prayer time. All of life is prayer and reminds me not to simply escape this world, but immerse myself in it, become incarnate in the whole world -- the pain of people, the beauty and cries of nature, the poverty of meaning -- all the while being who I am residing in the holy I AM."

Experiences of Contemplative Prayer

Dan describes a formative experience of contemplation that was unsought and only recognized years later. Here is how he describes the experience: "As a 19-year old student in Cupertino, California, I remember walking alone on the campus of De Anza College late one fall Sunday afternoon. All of a sudden, I was struck by the *presence* of the afternoon sun on the brown stucco walls and the deep silence of the place. I stopped walking. I had been jerked fully into the present moment, aware, expectant, alive, where I remained for several minutes in inner stillness and wonder. The sunlight seemed to burst forth; the air seemed filled with a vibrating energy. At the time my overwhelming feeling was one of awe and gratitude in being alive. I sensed inwardly the profound preciousness and sacredness of life. At the time, my theological framework had no room or explanation for such an experience, especially one that occurred outside the church walls. Towards what did this experience point, and where was it leading me? Awe was the one word that best describes what I felt that Sunday afternoon. I remember thinking that if I could answer these questions about that experience, I might someday write a book entitled *Beyond Awe*."

Patricia's experience of contemplation is not too different from many of us who are just beginning. She relates: "I have a hard time with contemplative prayer when I am alone. My most powerful experiences have been in a group that sits in silence and listens for God. Silence with others is somehow a deeper silence. I am more likely to have images from God rather than thoughts when I wait in a group in prayerful silence. I also have very strong images when I am in the silence with my companions. In my private attempts with contemplative prayer, I experience feelings of peace and also of unrest during my time of contemplation. After one experience, I had the strong urge to write a letter to my father and tell him what a wonderful father he had been to me. I have felt a lot of guilt over not going to see him often enough, but in this instance I felt God gave me a clear message that visits were not the only way to connect with him. The letter that I wrote deepened our relationship, and I think gave us both a new sense of peace about our relationship."

Imagine this person's experience of contemplation. "My personal experiences of contemplation have been most often centered in meditation on God's Word or while reading the writings of spiritual writers like Thomas Merton and Carlo Carretto.

"A few years ago restlessness took up residence in my soul. Something was missing in my relationship with Christ. As I look back now, I see that it was a dry time, a time of hunger and thirst, and a time of change. God began opening doors into spiritual living that I did not know existed. I was introduced to writers who candidly and beautifully wrote of their pursuit of God in terms that were unfamiliar to me. Even so, something in me recognized the territory they described as home, a place I wanted to abide. My soul responded as a baby to her mother's milk. I was ravenous. I continue to be fed and blessed by these writers, but am aware I need to step into the desert for myself. I want to have times when I am able to leave reason and desire for knowledge at the door and enter into God's presence as an empty and open vessel. I suspect this might be the treasure of contemplative prayer."

Consider how contemplation affects every aspect of life: One of my friends relates these experiences: "I feel like contemplation is God's gift to me when I am able to receive it. It sometimes feels like a time of God's Spirit imprinting me, an increased consciousness of my part in the shaping process. I know God is the initiator and that I am a responder. In addition to this imprinting, I have a few 'noticings' in my contemplative time: physical sensations like throbbing through my veins (different from relaxation), heart warmth, a sense of heaviness or the substance of God around me like a 'gel;' emotions: generally a radiant love for God and everyone in the world, a sense of 'oneness' with God and others…connection to all of creation; thoughts like 'this is what I'm here for', God is here, this is why he made me.

"I occasionally experience dialogue with God. This is simple and is generally about a discernment question in my life.

"I have images, generally of Jesus with me, but sometimes other symbols and stories that come into my mind like a movie.

"I find myself being at my best for spiritual direction or teaching, etc. when I am aware of this contemplative exchange with God."

The contemplative experience of this woman touches many dimensions of the spiritual life in a way that is both encouraging and enticing. Another soul-friend shares deeply a different kind of experience that moves me. She has passed through some deep, dark places in the inner confines of the soul to arrive at a place of unity with God. Her way of speaking of contemplation can be instructive for all. She says, "I find it difficult to report what happens in contemplation; I can't say what happens. It is beyond words, beyond my understanding and awareness. I rest in God and God adores me. I only know a bit about the time right before I enter into contemplation, and I know a little about the time right after my contemplation. Sometimes I don't think my contemplation of God ends as I move into the day; I seem to remain in a heightened awareness of God's living presence in everything and everyone. Beauty, suffering, and my fellow human beings bring me to tears more readily. I see God in the other more easily. Everyone, every stranger, even an enemy, an old building, or a part of nature is alive, vibrant, and pulsing.

"I find my body more electric, my senses more heightened, and my passions expansive. Continuous prayers of thanksgiving and intercession become like breathing out and breathing in. This is my experience of contemplation in action. Right before I am lost in God in prayer, it feels like I am floating in a pool of water or a warm lake -- my ears underwater, my body buoyant. It is night, and when I look up into the darkness and notice the piercing stars, I am swept up into the night and disappear. I am not aware of my body; there is no distinction between my body and the rest of the world that exists. There is no time.

There is only the eternal NOW. Sometimes a few minutes might pass, but it seems like a year or days might pass and it seems like an hour. There is no sense of chronos time."

Problems Praying Contemplatively

Most of us can identify with this confession: "My chief problems in praying contemplatively are two, and they are related. The most immediate problem I have is stilling the mind. Buddhists have a descriptive name for this phenomenon – 'monkey mind' – a habitual grasping one thought after another in rapid succession, an incessant inner dialogue with the self, complete with running commentary. How can God get a word in edgewise if I am engaged in such constant self-chatter? The more general problem that I have with contemplative prayer is lack of time, which is to say, a lack of discipline and commitment. Father Thomas Keating, in teaching Centering Prayer, recommends a minimum of twenty minutes twice a day. One of the major benefits of this discipline is its effect on taming the 'monkey mind,' of allowing one to experience deeper and longer periods of inner stillness. Thus, although contemplation is experienced as a gift, and although we can receive this gift without intentionally seeking it (as I did at age 19), we must have the discipline to cultivate stillness if we wish to drink from these waters more consistently."

An honest soul confesses, "My chief problem in praying contemplatively is simply taking the time to do it. When I get up in the morning, I keep thinking throughout the day, I'll get to it, but I don't. I find it difficult to empty my head when I have a lot going on or when I am worried about something. I can take time to read devotional literature or study the Bible, because both of these practices distract me from my splintered mind. But contemplation requires silence and emptying and I am rarely able to shift gears during my day. I find it time consuming to keep pushing thoughts from my head; I get into an internal battle trying to empty my mind and become present to God. I'm trying too hard, I know, but that's honestly what I find myself doing. At times I get the notion that I am too rational or practical to truly contemplate."

How many of us could acknowledge an overactive mind in our effort to pray contemplatively? "The biggest barrier to my prayer is I, me, myself! Disciplining my mind to be quiet, letting go of the desire for knowledge, and putting down the mirror I use to observe myself praying is all going slowly for me. I am still convinced that it is important for me to continue to keep my daily appointments with God and to remember that contemplative prayer in its essence is not something I do, but is a gift of grace. My hunger for God is always being tested by the demands of life. I have far to go in keeping boundary lines drawn that protect my time in Abba's arms."

Some persons have found that reading or praying a psalm has been good preparation for contemplation. One of my friends says, "Reading the Psalms devotionally for the past several years has been transformative for me. They give words to the cries of my heart, whether of pain or praise, and center my hopes in God alone. Until only recently, the richness of the Psalms had eluded me. The Spirit continues to open them in ways that I could not have imagined. To see my Savior on every page has filled me with hope and praise. For this, I am grateful!"

One person listed a few problems that people on the contemplative path often have:

Trying to hard.

Seeking contemplative experiences above all else.

Talking about the contemplative experience too much.

Reading and trying to follow too many books about contemplative prayer.

Hopes for Contemplation

Perhaps these questions and cautions uttered by someone faithfully on the journey should guide all of our hopes and expectations regarding contemplative prayer: How can I bring God glory? How can I be more fully the creation God has created me to be? How can I love more deeply? Suffering more quietly?

I do not think it is good to put expectations on God. Wherever God takes me, I'm surrendered. Whatever God wants, I will do. If God wishes to take this type of prayer away, all will be well. I am God's.

Can you imagine the following vision springing out of the deep silence of contemplation? "I have had far more success with contemplative prayer in a community setting. I have loved sitting with friends listening for God's Voice. The silence is heaven sent! I had many doubts about the practice of listening for a word from God for another person without any knowledge of their situation. What actually happens during these moments of listening is beyond explanation. I found many of the experiences to be so grace-filled that my desire to understand was not important. Gratitude is the most frequent response. My mind races at the thought of what it would be like if all Christians practiced corporate contemplative prayer."

Consider this open confession of one man's hopes for his life of contemplation. "Considerable scientific evidence now documents the many beneficial effects on health, well-being, and capacity to love through stilling the mind in meditation and contemplation. While I would hope to reap some of those benefits, they are not my primary motivation for seeking to deepen my practice of contemplative prayer. Rather, I am drawn to contemplation primarily to deepen my relationship with God. Specifically, I seek to move beyond a primarily intellectual awareness of God to a relationship of the heart. In addition, I hope that by being faithful in contemplative practice, I will become increasingly aware of my own inner (i.e., true) self- awareness of God's love for that self, and through it my own connectedness with all of God's creatures. I hope that this awareness will allow me to love God and my fellow humans more fully, more purely, and with less attachment. I hope that I will find more joy and that I will learn to be fully present to the life that I am living daily. Through the inner work of contemplation I hope that the fruit of the Spirit becomes more evident in my life."

I do love the way that some persons can come straight to the point. Here is one example: "I just hope I can get to the place where I can say that I have a contemplative life. If I ever can say this, I hope that I can reflect God's purpose in every aspect of my life."

Perhaps one of the capstones of our expectations and hopes might sound like this: "My expectations are high because God is a great and awesome God! I desire nothing more than a whole and undivided heart for God. I hope to learn to love others as He loves me and to become free from self-interest as my motivation. I want to be simple on the inside and open on the outside. I hope that I can learn to trust God enough to accept the 'fiery darts' of the devil in a way that God is revered and honored.

"I find that the first two verses of Psalm 131 do speak directly of my desires:

'O LORD, my heart is not lifted up,
  my eyes are not raised too high;
  I do not occupy myself with things
  too great and too marvelous for me.
  But I have calmed and quieted my soul,
  like a weaned child with its mother;
  my soul is like the weaned child that is with me'."

An Account of One Person's Metamorphosis

Another daring soul shared with me an account of her extended afternoon and evening of contemplation. It is a description of mindfulness; it is an example of self-awareness; it is the kind of experience that people have when they are open to the moment, to God. I hope you can delight in this adventure of the spirit.

"This afternoon I have been walking in the garden at St. Joseph's. As usual, I was drawn to each area of planting to take in the fragrance and enjoy the rich color of the various flowers, the tiny magenta ones planted around the phone pole, the deep violet of one last iris, the rich pinks and brilliant whiteness of the clumps of peonies, the pastel pink and orchid impatiens, and the bright yellow English daisies planted with the red-orange begonias and the red-green grasses. I finally wandered up the path lined with the silver-gray trunks of huge sycamore trees and sat down on a particular green bench, my favorite spot along the walkway.

"I was especially aware of the cool breezes today that crossed my face and the grasses and branches bending in the wind. I was filled with peace and contentment and a lightness of spirit, which I have been experiencing for some time, but today these emotions were accompanied by a sudden sense of complete freedom.

"I was content to feel the breeze, watch the wind moving through the branches and the clouds gliding across the sky, admiring all that surrounded me and praising God for all of creation – its beauty, its complexity, its diversity. The sense of absolute freedom continued within me. I had no cares, no burdens, no schedule to follow; the day was mine.

"It was then that I saw a butterfly gracefully progressing from spot to spot. Suddenly I realized that I, too, was one of God's butterflies, and that I felt as weightless and free to move within God's creation as that butterfly. The realization suddenly came to me that I was like the butterfly in other ways.

"I had started out as a scrawny, serious, quiet child – much like a caterpillar. Feeling that I had been created to learn, to absorb knowledge, I nibbled away at the leaves of book after book, consuming the knowledge of the pages as the caterpillar consumes the tender leaves and stems of plants, storing them away as food for the next stage of its life. I stored away knowledge in the same fashion.

"As the caterpillar spins itself into a cocoon and enters the second stage of its development, I was wrapped tightly by the threads of my own anxieties and was confined or restricted by my feelings of insecurity and inadequacy. I entered the next stage of my life, as an educator, in a rather constricted environment—my own cocoon. I had never been a fledgling bird that tried its wings and flew off into the world to become more social and move about from place to place. I never strayed far away from a classroom. I had been the tiny, inconspicuous bookworm too long. Time passed, and my cocoon became more comfortable now, shutting out relationships and encapsulating me in a cocoon of self-reliance and independence.

"I suppose that the caterpillar is unaware of the progression of changes that occur in the process God has developed by which the tiny creature so tightly bound in its silken capsule is to emerge into its third stage of life. At first I, too, was unaware of the fact that although I was still confined I was also changing. The intellect which I had so persistently fed and exercised and which was the part of me that I strived to develop began to lose its dominating power, and feelings, so long repressed by intellectual determination, began to make their presence known. Emotions became stronger and more frequently broke through to be expressed. The warm heart, which had been secluded within me, began to allow its warmth to be exposed and shared with others.

"I thought that all of this was transpiring as part of my plan, and that I was in control. But then growth began to occur and expand within my spirit. Filled gradually with the fruits of the spirit, such as love, joy, peace, faith, etc., my soul continued to expand. Little by little the threads of anxiety and the walls of doubt, independence, and self-reliance began to weaken and break.

"As a student I had studied the metamorphosis of the butterfly, and as a teacher I had taught that progressive system of development to many others. Today I suddenly realized that I also had experienced a metamorphosis. I, too, according to God's plan and God's grace have been transformed. I know that I am one of God's children, but today I felt like one of God's butterflies. There was buoyancy, a lightness of spirit, a freedom that made me feel that I was completely free to wander about in God's garden, the garden of God's creation.

"I realized that I have been particularly blessed, and I am freer than the butterfly nearby in that I have flown to gardens and spots of grandeur to witness God's creation on six continents. I have been fortunate to visit not only the natural wonders of the world, but also many of its man-made wonders. I have been privileged to meet and talk with many of God's children scattered all over the world. I have broken out of the confines of my limited existence, and warmed by God's love, filled with God's peace, and more recently empowered by increased trust in God's abiding presence, I am as free as the butterfly before me to move about, unencumbered and filled with joy.

"I don't have brilliant colors or gossamer wings to capture attention. But I hope that there are other markings that are visible. I pray that the radiance of God's love may be seen within me, and that compassion, gentleness, and patience show through.

"Tonight I reluctantly left the garden to drive to a church service. The hymns in the service turned out to be old favorites. Surprisingly a phrase in one hymn and the theme of the sermon were 'He touched me'. Tears filled my eyes as I realized that God had created me, and Christ had touched me. I felt like the woman in the reading of the evening scripture who had been suffering from an illness for many years and had been searching for healing. Seeing Jesus in the crowd she reached out to him and touched his robe. I have been suffering and praying for wholeness. I had been longing for a relationship with God hoping that it would heal the feelings of loneliness and periods of despair that I have often experienced. I, too, had at last reached out to Christ, and at the same time he reached towards me and touched me. Now a general feeling of well-being fills me. I feel light and weightless. I have been transformed from the scrawny, silent bookworm into a being who is unburdened, light-hearted in spirit, and free.

"I wanted to pray. Often when I begin to pray, the words that come to mind are from hymns or anthems. Tonight was no exception. This time the words were from a Taize song. 'Thank you, Lord ... been so good ... been my friend ... been my light ... been my peace ... been my joy.' I pray you will be my life. I just want to thank you, Lord.'

Does not an experience like this one cause us to ask: "What is this strange but compelling path? What is this way to which you feel drawn and cannot turn back?"

What does this word, "contemplation," mean? You may look it up in a dictionary, search for it in contemplative literature, or ask a saint about contemplation, and still not get a satisfactory answer. You only know contemplation when you are led into it.

3

A Stronger Grasp on Contemplation

Some things are indefinable and inexpressible. According to the mystics, contemplation is one of those things – you can't define it and you can't speak about it. This inhibition, however, has not stopped the endless flow of images and metaphors and books on the subject. How can we best define what we cannot even speak of? Perhaps we can best get at a richer understanding of contemplation through a spotted approach in a narrative mode. Here's what I mean.

Some years ago I took a course in "Projecting the Future" where the first class began with the professor saying, "I will not offer you a linear description of the unfolding future, but I will throw a few thoughts like mud on the wall and we will see what sticks." I propose to throw a few experiences on the screen and connect them with a narrative that ties them together. I will introduce you to those persons and books that have shaped my understanding and search for the path to contemplation. Since I agree with the mystics who say that you cannot define contemplation, you can only experience it, I hope that my accumulated experience will give you a few insights into contemplation.

In the first chapter I related my sense of call to the contemplative path, but it would be inaccurate to say that this is the beginning of my interest and experience in contemplation. My interest in a deeper relationship with God was awakened soon after my conversion to Jesus Christ through a book given me by a mentor. Throughout my sixty years of being on this journey, it seems that when I am prepared, the right person or book comes into my life. I think that it might be helpful for me to describe the circumstances of these events and to identify a few seminal thoughts in those books. This is my way of projecting a few images on the screen.

When I was eighteen years old, Dr. W. M. Ringsdorf gave me the first book that had a hint of contemplation, A *Testament of Devotion* by Thomas Kelly. Thomas Kelly was a Quaker who believed in the "inner light" and in the possibility of knowing God intimately. In the early pages of this book, he wrote that "deep within us all there is an amazing inner sanctuary of the soul, a holy place, a Divine Center, a speaking Voice to which we may continuously return."[1] This began to shape the notion that deep within me there was a place of meeting God, a place that was holy. It also suggested to me that in that sacred place there was a Voice that spoke to me. Many of the sentences in this book were far beyond my spiritual comprehension, yet there was a kind of current that seemed to run through its pages that magnetized and compelled me. Though I did not understand much of what I read, the notion of a center being within me where I could meet God and hear God's speech remained.

Kelly further spoke of the "slumbering Christ" within us who stirred to be awakened desiring to be clothed with earthly form and action. I mostly missed the meaning of this metaphor as well as the affirmation that "He (Christ) is within us all." About forty years passed before I began to realize the truth of this simple statement. For many years I also pondered a puzzling expression in Kelly's book – "the eternal now." Only as I got farther along the contemplative path did I realize the depth of this phrase. It points to the same experience as the quote from James Finley – "God is the metaphor for the infinity of the mystery the present moment manifests." How long did it take for that phrase to break open for me?

When I was a freshman in college, two other books appeared in my life: *The Practice of the Presence of God* by Brother Lawrence and *Letters by a Modern Mystic*, by Frank Laubach. Not too much is known about Brother Lawrence. He was a Frenchman born in poverty in Lorraine in 1611. At the age of eighteen, he was converted to Christianity. He became a soldier and then a servant to a wealthy family. In 1666 at the age of fifty-five he joined a Carmelite order where he became a lay brother.

During the years from his entry into the order and his death in 1691,

---

[1] Thomas Kelly, A *Testament of Devotion* (*San Francisco: Harper and Row*, 1941), *p*. 3.

he spent most of his time serving in a hospital kitchen. Those who lived with him and worked around him realized that he lived from a quiet center with a serene faith. After his death many people were interested in knowing about the faith and practice of this devout soul who so simply manifested the Spirit of Christ.

One of the most quoted lines from the pen of Brother Lawrence speaks of his continuous prayer: "My set times of prayer are not different from other times of the day."[2] This little man who had committed himself to Christ had so wedded his prayer with washing dishes and pots and pans that prayer and work were one. This devotion to work and to prayer formed one piece of fabric. He once said that "the shortest way to God is to go straight to him by a continual exercise of love and doing all things for his sake."

Very early Brother Lawrence helped me to see that the deepest spirit of prayer can be wedded, indeed, must be wedded to action. Those who think prayer is navel gazing, self-absorption, and withdrawal from life surely would be corrected by the simple testimony of this devoted brother.

Following the same pathway of prayer described by Brother Lawrence, Frank Laubach gave a contemporary expression for modern people. He was born in 1884 in the United States, but he was a citizen of the world. When he was forty-five years of age, he was serving as a missionary in the Philippines. In search of a deeper devotion to Christ, he often spent evenings on Signal Hill listening for God to speak to him through his own lips.

Like Brother Lawrence, Laubach also had perfectly joined his spiritual quest with his vocation. During the last forty years of his life, he traveled the world as an educator teaching illiterate people to read. His method was "each one teach one" and his way of teaching soon was embraced in many of the countries around the world. Many things can be said about him – "Man of the Year," author of over fifty books, greatest educator of modern times, and saint.

I first met Frank Laubach through his booklet, *Letters by a Modern Mystic*, which recorded the messages he heard on Signal Hill on the island of Mindanao and wrote them in letters to his father. I must have read this

---

[2] Gene Evans ed., *Practicing His Presence*. (Frank Laubach and Brother Lawrence) (Goleta, CA. Christian Books, 1973) pp. 55-56.

booklet a dozen times. In the evening he went behind his hut up on the hill and listened for God. He described how God spoke to him through his own lips, and then he rushed back to his hut to record what God had said. Something within me resonated with his daring commitment, his struggles, and his lofty vision of living before God and looking at the world and all the people through God's eyes.

In 1956 I had an opportunity to have dinner with Laubach. I was so full of admiration of him, his achievements and his life in God that I could hardly ask him any questions. The hours I spent with him that evening deepened his mark on me. There lingers in my memory his testimony: "If there is any contribution that I have to make to the world that will live, surely it must be my experience of God on Signal Hill."[3]

His listening to God speak to him through his own lips inspired me during my college days, and afterward his example gave me courage to write in my journal what I believed God said to me in prayer. In prayer I learned to listen quietly and then to ask, "What would you say to me today?" Strangely, something always came to mind to record.

The next book that would eventually shape my spiritual journey was *The Cloud of Unknowing* written by an English monk in the fourteenth century giving advice to a serious seeker for God. The first time that I read this book I made it through about ten pages before I tossed it aside. I could pronounce the words and read the sentences, but I had no earthly (or heavenly) idea what the author meant. Several times over the next few years, I picked up the book and tried to read it, but got nowhere. Approximately forty years later, I began to read one tiny section each day (1 to 2 pages); I meditated on the words and sought to incorporate his message into my prayer with little success. Ten years later, after I had felt called to follow the contemplative path, I began to understand "darkness of faith," "the way of unknowing," and "a naked intent for God." There is an old saying that "when the student is ready, the teacher will appear." Sometimes the teacher precedes our readiness, as my experience of *The Cloud of Unknowing* suggests.

Thomas Merton has been one of those companions in the spirit that has shaped my understanding of contemplation. He first entered my life when I was about forty-six years of age. He came to me in the text

---

[3] *Ibid.*, p. 9.

of New Seeds of Contemplation. Of course, I had heard of Merton prior to that era, but I had never seriously read his writings. This book came recommended by Father Gus (Augustine) who at the time was the Retreat Master at the Monastery of the Holy Spirit at Conyers, Georgia. He had been Abbott of the monastery for a number of years, but had been given less responsibility as the retreat master when he grew older. Father Gus had been a novice with Merton at the Abbey of Gethsemani in Kentucky. I delighted in hearing all of Gus's Merton stories.

Merton challenged my thinking; he was a master at asking questions. For example, "What one of you can enter into himself and find the God Who utters him?" Such a question presumes that our existence depends upon God's utterance, and it also questions our ability to find the God who utters us. Merton asserts that none of us can withdraw into ourselves and find this God whom we seek. He says, "No natural exercise can bring you into vital contact with Him. Unless He utters Himself in you, speaks His own name in the center of your soul you will no more know Him than a stone knows the ground upon which it rests in its inertia."[4]

Merton wrote prolifically about contemplation and the journey to the center of the soul. He explored nearly every facet of the false ego and its efforts to justify itself; he exposed the false ego's efforts to keep us from discovering and realizing our true self. Silence, too, is essential for the deeper knowledge of God. In too many instances our mental and verbal prayers are ways of avoiding a confrontation with the false self. This kind of prayer only briefly covers our anxiety. Though helpful at this stage of my journey, Merton never grasped me with a firm grip for another twenty years. Only after the call to contemplation and the role of Contemplative Prayer in that call did I become a Merton Junkie.

In the 1980's Jean-Pierre de Caussade became my guide through Abandonment to Divine Providence. Once again, Father Gus pointed me to this director of souls. Father Gus knew the book well. When he had been a monk at Gethsemani, the Abbott assigned him this book to read and reflect on for a year. When his appointment with the Abbott came the following year, the Abbott assigned him a second year to live with this book. Finally, after directing him to meditate on the ideas in this

---

[4] Thomas Merton, New Seeds of Contemplation. (New York: New Directions Publishing Corporation, 1961), p. 39.

book for three years, Gus was given a new assignment. "If the Abbott discerned that this book was that important for one of his monks, surely it must hold a message for me," I reasoned.

Jean-Pierre de Caussade lived and wrote in the seventeenth century. We know about him through letters that he wrote. Over a period of several years he wrote spiritual directions to nuns. His letters were preserved and published a hundred and ten years after his death. All of his letters have a common theme: God's will is revealed in the things that come to us; we are to do God's will in the present moment. This emphasis is capsulated in a short phrase – "the sacrament of the present moment."

Fundamental to de Caussade's direction is the conviction that God still speaks to us today as God spoke to our ancestors. He urged: "To be faithful to the design of God, this comprises the whole of one's spiritual life."[5] I became so enthralled with the lessons in his letters that I spent six months writing my own meditation on each of them. He discovered dozens of ways and adopted numerous analogies and metaphors to urge the reader to attend to God "in the present moment." Absorbing his guidance during those months implanted within me the realization that my spirituality took shape in the present moment. Listening for God, realizing the presence of God, and obeying God always occur in the present moment.

Another guide to me, perhaps the most helpful guide, in the latter years of my life has been a lay brother who belonged to the Little Brothers of Jesus, Carlo Carretto. Brother Carlo came into my life in a strange and providential way. One of the publishing houses sent me a catalogue. As I had done so often, I skimmed the pages of the catalogue to see what it offered in Christian Spirituality. As my eyes ran down the page, my vision was halted by the name of a book – *Letters from the Desert*. Yes, Brother Carlo was the author. I was compelled to order the book. I received it and in packing for a trip to Arkansas, stuck it in my brief case.

On Saturday morning, I took the book to breakfast with me and seated in a booth waiting for my food, I began reading the introduction. The opening words grabbed me and would not let me stray from the reading

---

[5] Jean-Pierre de Caussade, *Abandonment to Divine Providence*. (Garden City, New York: Image Books, 1973), p. 22.

until I had read each of Carlo's meditations. These were the words that fastened themselves to my mind: "The call of God is mysterious, it comes to us in the darkness of faith ..." These words had a ring of authenticity and a magnetism that gave birth to a mentor relationship with Carlo. Here is a portion of his testimony that bears witness to his contemplative life:

I thought the knowledge of God I was acquiring through study and reasoning was the real and only one. I hadn't yet understood that it was only an image, a covering, an introduction to God's true and authentic revelation, which is supernatural and eternal. God is unknowable, and only he can reveal himself to me through ways which are wholly his, unrepeatable in words and in concepts beyond our understanding.

So true prayer demands that we be more passive than active; it requires more silence than words, more adoration than study, more concentration than rushing about, more faith than reason. We must understand thoroughly that true prayer is a gift from heaven to earth, the Father to his child; from the Bridegroom to the bride, from he who has to him who has not, from Everything to nothing.[6]

This brief introduction to Brother Carlo gives you a sense of his contemplative spirit and his amazing spiritual insight. I ordered all his books and devoured them like a man breaking fast. His metaphors stimulated my imagination, his intimacy with God evidenced on every page of his writings nurtured my spirit, and his encouragement to let go of everything that distracted me from God met with my response. After living with Brother Carlo for a decade, I made a pilgrimage to Spello, Italy to feel his hands upon my head and hear the prayer for me he uttered.

In the early 1990s, Father Thomas Keating became a guide to me. I first began to hear about Father Keating after he came to the Monastery of the Holy Spirit to direct seminars in Centering Prayer. Centering prayer is a form of contemplative prayer. It was named and developed by Keating to provide a less forbidding way to enter into contemplation.

Before deciding to become a monk, Thomas Keating was a bright young student in Berkeley, California who had an interest in both Christian contemplation and Eastern mysticism. He seriously studied both of these approaches. After making a decision for the religious life, he entered St. Joseph's Abbey located near Spencer, Massachusetts.

---

[6] Carlo Carretto, *Letters from the Desert.* (Maryknoll, New York: Orbis Books, 1973), pp. 55-56.

After becoming the Abbott of St. Joseph's monastery, he became aware of a growing hunger for the experience of God in a number of young people. He noted a number of young people turning toward the east to find their spirituality. Since he understood both the eastern and western approaches to contemplation, he decided to offer these seekers a form of contemplative prayer that was more accessible to persons who lived outside the walls of a monastery. He called this type of contemplation "Centering Prayer."

This form reduces the obstacles to contemplative prayer. He invites seekers to drop all thoughts in the act of continuously turning to God. This is possible outside the monastery where practitioners do not have the benefit of a structured life of prayer like the monks. This form of prayer refines one's intuitive faculties and turns the attention from the ordinary flow of thoughts. Contemplative prayer consists of letting go of every thought and tuning into a deeper level of reality.[7] Keating recommends two daily sessions of twenty minutes to practice the centering exercise. His instructions make room for struggle, failure, and beginning again. I have found the simplicity of Centering Prayer a helpful way to get on the contemplative path.

In addition to Father Keating three other spiritual personalities have aided the movement of centering prayer. These three persons are Basil Pennington, Father Tom Francis and Cynthia Bourgeault. I never met Father Basil Pennington, though for a time he was the Abbott at the Monastery of the Holy Spirit. I entered his classroom through his book on centering prayer. He gave me one very valuable insight.

In analyzing the kinds of thoughts that distract us in the silence of centering prayer, he called special attention to the distraction of the "monitor."[8] The monitor observes the experience of prayer while it is occurring so that afterward it may say that it was a good meditation or a poor meditation. Making a judgment like this indicates that the one praying has one eye on God and the other on the self, a divided consciousness. Pennington urges us to keep both eyes upon God and to forget the self and type of experience that we are having.

---

[7] Thomas Keating, *Open Mind, Open Heart*. (New York: Continuum. 1994), pp. 34-36.

[8] Basil M. Pennington, *Centering Prayer: Renewing an Ancient Christian Prayer Form*. (New York: Image Books, 1980), p. 104.

When I read about the monitor, I knew immediately that simultaneously I had been praying and watching myself pray. The call to focus both eyes upon God, when I am able to do it, enables me to forget my self and to give up evaluating my experience. In the silence of prayer being with God is crucial no matter what the experience is like. The admonitions of Pennington have created in me a desire to let go of everything in my prayer but God, yet I still struggle with the intrusions of the monitor.

Father Tom Francis is a monk at the Monastery of the Holy Spirit. He has been a friend and confidant to me on more than one occasion. When I go on retreat or take groups to the monastery, I make an effort to converse with Tom Francis. If I am leading a group, I try to get him to speak with them. Recently, when I accompanied a group of men to the monastery from the church that I attend, I asked him to meet with us and to talk with us about centering prayer. He gladly accepted the opportunity and provided us notes on his view.

Tom Francis has a wonderful way of describing centering prayer that lacks the trappings of the theological grounding and the psychological implications, though he is fully aware of both. In utter simplicity he speaks about being present to Jesus, waiting for him in the silence and being taken into the communion of the Godhead during meditation. His talks have a matter of fact tone that helps the group glide along with him like a skier on snow. He is not so rigid about the practice of prayer. Tom Francis admonishes us to "do what you can."

I am indebted to Tom Francis for introducing me to Cynthia Bourgeault, an Episcopal priest, who has written an excellent book on centering prayer, *Centering Prayer and Inner Awakening*. Once when I was at the monastery for a day's retreat, Tom Francis told me that he had just finished editing Cynthia's book, and he urged me to purchase a published copy. Cynthia Bourgeault spent several years as a hermit at Snow Mass, Colorado studying the writings of Father Thomas Keating. During those years a monk named Raphael, whose friendship was transformative, mentored her. His death proved to be a terrible loss.

In her book she emphasizes that centering prayer is not about sublime states of consciousness or mystical experiences, but about transformed daily life. This transformation helps you "to be a bit more present in your

---

[9] Cynthia Bourgeault, *Centering Prayer and Inner Awakening*. (Cambridge, Massachusetts: Cowley Publications, 2004), p. 30.

life, to be a bit more flexible and forgiving with those you live and work with, more honest and comfortable in your own being."[9] After reading her book, I had an opportunity to hear her speak during a retreat. In listening to her words, I had the sense that she spoke from both the depth of self-knowledge and the knowledge of God. She was in her speech, response, and demeanor what she had written about.

I wrote earlier about the impact that Merton's *New Seeds of Contemplation* had on me and about picking up a copy of *Contemplative Prayer* after the mentor retreat. Merton returned as my teacher for a year. I not only read the book *Contemplative Prayer* but I also read his biography and other writings like *Zen and the Birds of Appetite* and *The Inner Experience: Notes on Contemplation*, which was published after his death. Because of the density of *The Inner Experience*, I asked a group of friends to gather on Sunday evenings to discuss it. We took turns leading the discussion as we sought to understand his view of contemplation, the true self, the false self, and the social implications of contemplation.

Merton defines contemplation theologically as an expression of Christ in us. He explains that Christ is not to be present in us merely as a memory or a model or a good example. While it is true that the Divine Nature infinitely transcends our nature, in Christ this gap between God and us humans has been bridged. God came among us in Christ; God took upon Godself our nature. Even more explicitly, Merton says, "Christ is really present in us, more present than if he were standing before us visible to our bodily eyes. For we have become 'other Christs'."[10]

One of the ways that we enter into the immediate presence of God according to Merton is through the true self. He suggests:

"In Christianity the inner self is simply a stepping stone to an awareness of God. Man is the image of God, and his inner self is a kind of mirror in which God not only sees Himself, but also reveals Himself to the 'mirror' in which He is reflected. Thus, through the dark, transparent mystery of our own inner being we can, as it were, see God 'through a glass.' All this is of course pure metaphor. It is a way of saying that our being somehow communicates directly with the Being of God, Who is 'in us.'"[11]

---

[10] Thomas Merton, *The Inner Experience*. (San Francisco: Harper Collins, 2003), p. 46.
[11] *Ibid.*, p. 11.

In this description of the inner experience Merton invited me to take a step inward in search of my true self, which is created in the image of God. He likens this inner self to a mirror that reflects to God God's own being. And while God sees God's Self in our true being, we also get a glimpse of God through the mysterious darkness of our inner self. In these moments when God presents God's Self to us, our being communicates directly with the being of God.

With painful persistence Merton seeks to help us understand that the true self is not the ego, it is not a separate entity, but it is the entirety of our being before God. He says, "The inner self is not a part of our being, like a motor in a car. It is our entire substantial reality itself, on its highest and most personal and most existential level. It is like life, and it is life: it is our spiritual life when it is most alive...It is in and through and beyond everything that we are...It is a new and indefinable quality of our living being."[12]

Do I understand the depths of these statements? No. I cannot make the claim to understand them; yet each of the words and phrases point me toward a reality that I already intuit. When I read these paragraphs, I have the sense that Merton is taking me by the hand and leading me into my own depths, which when cleared of clutter take me down the path to the contemplation of God.

Soon after my earlier encounter with Merton through New Seeds of Contemplation, James Finley came to me through an early book, Merton's Palace of Nowhere. Finley is a psychotherapist, a teacher, retreat leader, and writer. My experience of learning from Finley's writings has been somewhat odd. I struggled and struggled with Merton's Palace of Nowhere and finally stopped reading it. I could never get into the message. Isn't it strange how you must be ready for a book before it can speak to you? Years later after I received this call into contemplation, Finley spoke loudly to me and I read and underlined in red every book of his that I could find.

For five or six years, Merton served as Finley's novice master. Through his relationship with Merton, he began to discover the path of contemplation. Like Merton, Finley has benefited from Zen and weaves it into his contemplation.

---

[12] Ibid., p. 6.

I derived two particular helpful insights into the practice of contemplation from Finley. He says "contemplation is a state of realized oneness with God. When engaged in contemplation, we rest in God resting in us. We are at home in God at home in us."[13] As I thought about the aspect of rest in contemplation, a circular image came into my mind. I am resting in God – God is resting me – who is resting in God! I began to repeat this simple affirmation in my walks: "Resting in God who is resting in me who is resting in God!" With this recitation I began to feel myself settling ever more deeply into the rest of God.

Another idea of Finley's regarding contemplation has become instructive. He speaks of "the divinity of what just is." He explains this daring assertion:

"By this is meant the primitive intuitive knowledge ... the quiet inner assurance, that the present moment, just the way it is, is in its deepest actuality, a manifestation of the divine. Our initial point of experiential access to the divinity of the present moment is found in our moments of spontaneous contemplative experience. In such moments we are instantaneously transformed in being awakened to the way we deep down really are, one with the way the present moment deep down really is."[14]

This view of reality is radically different from the positivist view that the world is flat, directionless, and meaningless. Finley encourages us to believe that the very ordinary things that appear in our lives every day manifest the divine. With an awakened heart we get glimpses and intuitions of the spiritual depth of the world in which we live.

Called to be a Contemplative?

On this amazing journey I have learned from others and from my own experience that you don't simply decide to be a contemplative. You are called to be a contemplative. I have asked, "When was I called to be a contemplative?" Was I called to be a contemplative in the first few years of my Christian life when A *Testament of Devotion* and *The Practice of the Presence of God* fell into my hands? Or, was my interest in living continuously in the presence of God merely nurtured by these devotional writers?

---

[13] James Finley, *The Contemplative Heart.* (Notre Dame, Indiana: Sorin Books, 2000), p. 17.

[14] *Ibid.*, p. 19.

When I take a long look back, I think my early experiences indicated my destiny. What happened to me at the monastery just a few years ago and the subsequent confirmation that I have received, seem much more like a call, and its persistence has strengthened this conviction.

The call that came to me in 2002 has inspired me to read broadly in the field of contemplation. Furthermore, the call has led me to reflect on my studies as well as my experiences, to discuss this journey with friends, and to practice regularly an effort to enter the deep silence. I do believe that searching out the pathway to contemplation has been God's work in my life; it is a vocation that I did not choose; it chose me. All that has occurred in my previous journey has been preparation for this serious endeavor. As I offer this interpretation as testimony, I am very much aware that not everyone comes to contemplation in the same manner. Your call and your entrance into this way will be unique. You are to discern and follow your calling.

Our trusted guides tell us that there are numerous signs that indicate that God may be calling a person into a contemplative life. For example, when our old forms of prayer begin to dry up, when repeatedly our efforts to pray seem to take us nowhere, this may be preparation for taking a new pathway to God. Or, we may notice a growing desire for silence and inner stillness, a desire that leads us into contemplation. The kind of desire that would eventually lead us into our depths cannot be squelched; it persists through both our ignorance and resistance.

An attraction to reading books and articles on contemplation, a fascination with the subject, often suggests that God is preparing us to move forward. When the pursuit of this deeper life finds encouragement in reading and reflecting on the subject, we should pay attention to the hungers it awakens in us, and the direction toward which it is pointing. Even before we begin to read books on contemplation or approach the subject with friends, we may find ourselves being gently led along the contemplative path. We may even be practicing a type of contemplation before we have a name for it. Should this occur, our call would seem more like an awakening to a reality operative within us than a call coming from the outside.

In addition to these signs, the providential occurrences in your life provide a strong indication of God's beckoning into a more contemplative life. When the unplanned events of your life begin to awaken you to your hunger, when they point you in the direction of contemplation, they may constitute either a call or the confirmation of a call to this kind of life. Those confirming events in my life were the experience at the monastery, the purchase of a book by Merton, the meeting with a friend who loaned me Finley's lectures on contemplation, and my obsession with Finley's description of what "the present moment" manifests.

I invite you to wonder if you are being called into contemplation. Is this God's will for you? Is it the next step in your loving obedience? To engage in contemplation does not make you a greater Christian; it does not point you to a way higher than the average Christian; it does not make you a saint. But, quite simply, if God is calling you in this direction, it is the way for you to go. If you do not feel this call, lay this book down or give it to a friend, and proceed on your present course. On the other hand, if you feel the faint stirrings of an awakening, I invite you to join me on this contemplative journey. In the pages that follow I will share with you the experiences that I had in the early days of my journey, some of the biblical texts that have given rise to contemplation in me, and my reflections on a few of Merton's seminal ideas. I think of each of these short writings as starters for your periods of silence in God. As I have made my journey, I have wished for someone with whom I could walk. I hope that my sharing of thoughts and experiences with you will give you a sense of having a companion on your journey.

First Experiences

1. Testimony

The notion of Christian Contemplation entered my mind long before I heard the quote about the present moment; I feared contemplation. My fears fed on the perceived losses -- loss of words, loss of feelings, and loss of images. These losses, or the fear of such, caused me to hope that God would not lead me into contemplation. If contemplation did not include the familiar furniture of the House of Prayer, I had no pressing desire to go there.

God seemed to pay no attention to my anxieties. God has an agenda with each of us and nothing seems to shake it, not even our strong resistance. When the fullness of time came, God began moving in my life in an unexpected way. I experienced this movement as a call. Through the things that happened to me, God issued a call to contemplation. This call did not come to me in a flash with life-defining clarity, but it appeared in the confused state of my disheveled existence brought on by retirement. It came when I was passing from my established vocation into confusion about my identity and my future. This confusion was exacerbated by my sense of God's distance; God seemed absent from my struggle. What kind of call could this be in such messy circumstances?

I sought to ignore this transition by filling my calendar with engagements, as I had for two decades. But my effort to avoid facing my change in circumstance did not deter God's intention. My body spoke: persistent high blood pressure, congestive heart failure, shingles, and diabetes struck sequentially with little time between. God spoke in these events: "You are not to continue your life as usual." I was forced to make new decisions, which were preparatory for God's call.

A year later the Mentor's Retreat came. God spoke again. This tryst with the Spirit came like a stiff wind that filled the sail of my soul and set me in motion. I believe the freedom and joy that I began to experience confirmed God's call.

Picking up Merton's book, *Contemplative Prayer*, before leaving the monastery was not mere chance. God's call focused my attention on it and when I picked it up, I was drawn to its contents. I had no way of knowing at the moment that it would inform and explain to me the deepest hunger in my life. I read it like a famished worker; it nourished me, shaped me, and challenged me.

Within just a few days I received the tapes on Merton by James Finley and those words about the present moment containing both the manifest and the unmanifest mystery of God. God spoke to me through that metaphor and drew me more deeply into contemplative prayer. The pathway into contemplation seemed irresistible; it held a fascination from which I could not turn away; it completely seduced me and I willingly surrendered to its advances.

2. On Doubt

The choice to walk the path of contemplation exposed my soul both to radical doubt and unshakable trust. In contemplation doubt occurred when I lost confidence in old certitudes with their images and structures. Eventually those guarantees of certitude collapsed. As I began to experience God more directly, I realized that many of the structures of faith had become idols. In the absence of structure, doubt arises and chaos invades the soul. And doubt floats on the surface of chaos.

In the face of doubt my soul was overwrought with fear – fear that my life had been lived on a false premise, fear that God, after all, may not be there, and fear that my spiritual journey has taken me nowhere. In the face of paralyzing fear born of doubt, running back to rational thought held nothing. My old certitudes had been eroded and I was walking the way of 'unknowing.'

What then shall I do? Make friends with doubt and the fear it unleashes? Why did I not realize beforehand that the collapse of old structures of certitude would leave me extremely vulnerable to doubt? But at the same time, this loss made possible a new relationship with God based on trust alone. The old certitude depended on clinging to concepts and propositions that had now disappeared as a basis of knowledge. On this contemplative path, trust and trust alone unites the soul with God. This trust does not hinge on doctrine or dogma or on past experience, but upon God and God alone.

On the contemplative path, doubt becomes a friend and ally by teaching me that I must learn to trust God. And thus I find myself on a path that I have not chosen, led by a hand I cannot see, into a relationship with God over which I have no control.

3. Learning to be Still

Stillness, which sinks in after a long struggle, is a gift. Though we may work hard to get still and resolve repeatedly to keep our minds focused, this discipline cannot bring us to stillness. Stillness inexplicably comes to us as a present in the midst of our persistent efforts. After many fitful efforts, I am beginning to enter into a great stillness as a gracious gift. There must be many varied forms of stillness; my experience is like a great calm that wipes away fear.

The images of stillness that come to my mind include: a still cove at the lake, sometimes filled with waves and ripples from the boats or wind, but at the moment it lies quietly with a calm, still surface, mirror-like, perfectly reflecting white fluffy clouds floating in a rich blue sky. I see another image of stillness in a blue spruce standing tall in the monastery's garden of silence. In that same garden a brown thrasher shows me a picture of calmness as she sits motionless on a rail fence with her head cocked as though listening for a word from the wind. A memory floats into my mind of a leopard committed to long hours of stillness as she perches on a limb awaiting her prey.

T. S. Eliot knew about "the still point of the turning world." Even though the universe is constantly spinning, there is a still point at its center. The center of our center is by nature linked to the Center of All Things.

When I shed my tension like a snake sheds its skin, I feel my center slowing down from its busy turning and turning. And the Still Point of the turning world keeps attracting me like a magnet.

To find the stillness I must come to my center and feel its stillness, and then to be drawn into the stillness of the Center of All Things. Without effort or fear or struggle we can all let ourselves be drawn into this Center.

4. I Come Knocking

Over a number of decades, I have many times come to a door during meditation and prayer, searching for a handle that would open into contemplation.

I have come to this door by meditation on the scripture. At other times, the pathway has been silence and solitude. A few times the door has opened, and I have entered into fellowship with God. From that interaction with Holiness, I have felt fulfilled and empowered.

After all these years, I am still a novice in the deeper aspects of prayer. At times it appears to me that I am trying too hard. At other times it seems that I make more of contemplation than it deserves. In this moment I feel so ignorant of the way of God – the way of contemplation. I wonder if how far along we are with God really matters. Is it not enough that we are seriously on our way?

In my meditation, at an early hour of the day, I stood outside the door and knocked. I do not know if the Lord opened the door and invited me in or if his Spirit transported me to another place. I found myself on the cusp of time.

Contemplation meant standing there on the cusp of time as moments were being born, and realizing that God appeared in each successive moment. As the moments were born, God happened. Every moment manifested God as infinite mystery. And I, awed by the mystery, was invited to be present at the birthing of each moment, the manifestation of God in history.

As I am being called into God, I do not understand the Voice, and I do not know the way. So I remain there on the cusp of time waiting for God, looking for God, but I too seldom recognize the divine presence.

Yet, as I stand looking, I wonder if I get too close to see. While I am waiting for God contemplatively, the Presence enfolds me, and the intimacy is too close to distinguish.

5. Clarity on Contemplation

Contemplation is an act; it is gazing upon God whom we cannot see. Contemplation is a posture, one of quietly waiting. Contemplation is a practice, a constant return to the present moment, to see God in just what is. As I write these words, they sound like contemplation creates a very busy approach to God, and this would be an erroneous impression.

Contemplation is letting go; it is ceasing from my own busy activity in prayer; it is recognizing what already exists – God and I are one. This oneness is realized in letting go, in noticing, in gazing in the direction of the Holy, and in waiting, always waiting.

I value the days when I do not put much effort in contemplation. In those times of prayer, I seem to realize in a moment a sense of the divine. In those natural moments, I do not spend time seeking to control my thoughts, or suppressing my feelings, or neutralizing my imagination. In a strange and inexplicable way, I am "there," wherever "there" is. The simple awareness of the divine may not last long, sometimes only a moment, but that moment verifies the longed for reality of being in God.

Contemplation contains many states from an awakened desire for God to the consciousness of God in everything. Sometimes on this journey, the soul receives an infusion of the Holy in which it effortlessly swims in the presence of God in a sacred stillness. I seem to experience contemplation in many different forms, and this variety of realizations surely is part of God's infinite design. Especially in my later years the experience of God has become richer and more mature.

Contemplation may or may not lead to an infused union with God in which one is constantly aware of being embraced by the Presence. If this ever occurs in me, it will be because God has reached out to me, embraced me, and filled me with Godself. Such intimacy cannot be earned, and it is not under my control to gain or hold it. My discernment leads me along the pathway of contemplation until God chooses to draw me into Godself, into union of spirit with Spirit in the abyss of Love. Considering these insights and possibilities gives me great peace and delight.

6. Try Love

"You are trying too hard!" I seemed to hear those words in my mind as I had my regular walk in the neighborhood. To what do these words apply? Does it mean that I am endeavoring to get to a particular place in my contemplation? It could mean that I have a center, and in my silence I have imagined myself descending into this deep place where I hope to meet God. This descent to a "place" takes energy, and when I put forth this effort, it generates tension in me. Is this what it means to "try too hard"? I think so.

Tension gives evidence of "trying too hard." Clearing my mind of these efforts gets rid of the tension. I find that letting go and trusting the Spirit generally takes me where I am to be. Attending to the Spirit leads me into yet another aspect of contemplation.

At times I do not try very hard, sometimes not at all. There are days when I do not begin with quietness, other days also that I don't recollect myself and think of God's graciousness to me. Amazingly, on these days I am taken into the Presence. Maybe I am in training to learn to sit still in the Quiet without much, if any, effort at all.

What helps me most when I realize that I am trying too hard is to focus on the reality before me. God, whom I adore, resides in the moment, in the birthing of time, and when I come to this moment, God is present.

It takes little effort at all to be present to the moment. I say to myself, "Be where you are. Open your eyes to what is around you, and then consider the Mystery the material reality suggests. Realize you are united to the Divine."

7. Gentleness

"Be gentle with yourself." These words came to me once again on this journey; I welcomed the invitation to find times and places and ways to be gentle in my approach to contemplation. Since I cannot achieve the Ultimate Union with God in my own strength, why am I so hard on myself when I fail at the impossible?

Even more importantly, I follow him who issued an enduring invitation: "Come to me all who labor and are burdened...learn from me for I am gentle and humble and you will find rest of soul." (Matthew 11:28 paraphrased) He is gentle with parents who did not always understand his mission; he is gentle with disciples who doubt him, forsake him, and betray him. He is gentle with women who come seeking his help, and he is gentle with those who cannot believe he is risen from death. Surely he will be gentle with me and teach me the art of gentleness.

When and how do I wish to be gentle?

I would be gentle with myself when my regular time before God is rushed, too brief, or non-existent or seemingly a waste of time.

I would be gentle when I do not overcome old patterns of life that deny "the new creation."

I would be patient when my times of prayer end with a cold heart, restless hands, and feelings of being forsaken.

I would be gentle with myself when my actions betray my noble intentions.

I wonder if gentle souls do not more easily find the pathway into the Divine Presence. So I hope that you, O God, will not only show me mercy and gentleness, but that you make me a gentle and compassionate person.

8. Closing the Gap

"I in you and you in me."

I am beginning to understand, and in a small degree to experience, the closing of the gap between God and me. The gap, which sometimes feels like a gaping cavern, has created feelings of immense distance between God and me. In my earliest attempts at prayer, I pictured Christ at the right hand of God's throne, sitting there waiting to hear my prayer. During the intervening years the sense of distance has narrowed, but the "otherness" has remained.

I find myself perpetually yearning for an intimacy that dissolves the distance between his Spirit and mine. Whether this persistent desire lingers because of the matrix in which I first learned to relate to another person or whether it belongs to the finitude of the creature, I do not know the answer to my questions. Nevertheless I continue to experience a compelling urge, a hunger for intimacy with God. At one and the same time I desire to be my true created self without pretense, deceit or fear, and I also desire to experience God in me filling my world with holiness.

Contemplation makes clearer to me these life-directing longings. The contemplative way leads me beyond images and I-Thou relations and, hopefully, into a union that dissolves the distance. Jesus' statement, "I in you and you in me," is a metaphor that expresses the dissolution of this distance. In the mystery of his being in me and I in him my yearning finds rest, and the work of transformation occurs.

More often I find myself "centering" on him in me rather than approaching him as the Other. When this unity with him exists in prayer, another form of prayer simultaneously occurs. I believe that all the persons I love and all those who have requested my prayer, and even the children of God throughout the world are being prayed for through me. In a mystical way, I am in them and they are in me and Christ prays his prayer for them in me. In this way intercession occurs constantly as an integral part of contemplation. Though this is true, I still experience anxiety in the process of change.

9. Participation in God

Vaguely I recall Fr. Tom Francis of the Monastery of the Holy Spirit talking with me about his being taken into the life of the Holy Trinity. He spoke, as best I can recall, about being drawn into the love of the Father for the Son and the love of the Son for the Father through the Spirit. Through contemplation he affirmed his experience of personally participating in the dynamic life of the Trinity.

I was prepared neither theologically nor experientially to appreciate his excitement or the testimony he shared. At the time my image of God tended to be "wholly other" rather than the intimate Ground of Being. My prayer at best consisted of specific requests and an effort to listen for a word from God. Besides, my life at the time was so full of contradiction and ambiguity, I spent most of my energy trying to survive the day, and the idea of participation in the Godhead lay beyond the limits of my imagination. Because of these conflicts in thought and experience, Tom Francis' words lay dormant in me for a long time.

Groping my way along the path of contemplation, I occasionally hear vague murmurs of his testimony. While I understand the constant temptation to domesticate the Holy God by cheap familiarity, it need not occur in the sensitive soul. The Apostle John said, "...we share these things with you that you may have fellowship with us, and truly our fellowship is with the Father and with his Son, Jesus Christ." (I John 1:3).

John's purposive statement on the first hearing seems consistent with our standard theology. But when we translate koinonia as *"participation in,"* the emphasis changes. To participate means to engage in, to become part of someone or some event. St. Paul spoke of participation (koinonia) in the ministry and in the Body and Blood of Christ. Give your offering to this ministry, and through it you are there doing the work, participating in the outcome. Eat this bread and become the Body of Christ. Drink this wine and it becomes the lifegiving blood of Christ. Hear John's invitation! Enter into the life of the Apostle and into the life of God. Participate in the life of the community and in the life of God! Somehow I believe Saint John would have understood the testimony of Tom Francis.

10. Sitting Above Myself

The contemplative way leads through the land of mystery and surprise. One morning I set out on the road hoping that it would lead me to silence, and that in this silence I would perhaps hear the wordless Voice speaking to me in a manner that engaged me without informing me. Suddenly, I came to the land of surprise.

In the unfathomable silence at the Center, I noted that I seemed to be sitting above myself. It was as though I had a spiritual form exactly like my physical form, and this copy of the original was sitting in the same manner as my physical self, except about twelve inches above it. My feelings lay somewhere beyond relaxation and numbness. I noted my location without fear of exuberance.

I don't know how to estimate time in a period of intense encounter like this. Perhaps my awareness lasted sixty seconds or just a fleeting moment. How can I estimate this kind of time?

Is this brief out of the body experience of importance to a man like me on the Road to Contemplation? I really do not know. At the time I noted it with a ripple of amusement because in all my three score and ten years I had never sat above myself. And I found within myself a willingness to go on a journey into a larger space if the circumstance dictated it, but an astral projection seemed not to be my lot. So I settled down within myself, and the spiritual copy of me united with the original.

I believe it best not to think too much or too often about experiences like this. Preternatural experiences like this have little or nothing to do with the Spiritual journey. Given much attention they become distractions to the journey and to God.

11. On the Path

As I walk this path I am discovering a number of benchmarks, signs, or indications of change. These markers are not assurances or verifications of the maturity of my contemplation, but they are accidental changes and insights that have come to my attention. For example, when I sit down to contemplate, my body knows to get still. I can feel it immediately turning off as I begin to settle down. It's like the air suspension on my car, when the air is expelled and the auto settles down. My body does that. It settles into the chair, as if it knows why it is there without being told every time.

Invariably, my mind goes to my breath. I become conscious of how I am breathing – shallow or deep, slowly or a bit too rapidly. And after checking I usually forget about breathing altogether. I do keep breathing, but not consciously. (I wonder if that little forgetfulness might be a paradigm of contemplation. At first, I begin to desire God and move toward my depths, and as I traverse the path, I forget both the desire and the movement, but continue to do both.)

I always relax, but it does not yet become complete. I always notice a little pocket of tension after the initial settling, and I have to get settled again. Stillness comes as I strip off layers of tension.

With the tension gone I slide into a deep crevasse of peace. I am there "before" the Holy One. I say "before" to indicate my side of the relation, my offering myself to God, but the completion of the "before" depends upon God. And, some days I am conscious of the completion and on other days I am not. Whether conscious or not, the Holy God does the transformative work in me. I am coming to realize that contemplation is about transformation into my True Self, into God.

12. I Am Not Deluded

Since I do believe that we can be deluded in our efforts to know God and live in the Presence, I have wondered if I am deceived in following a way that I do not know. To some extent this question has persisted with me from the beginning. I think that it lurks on the edge of my consciousness because the contemplative way has for me turned everything upside down. Knowing becomes unknowing, seeing turns into unseeing and the pathway has no signs. How can I know that I am not deceiving myself in this journey?

In the midst of this serious questioning I asked my spiritual guide what she thought about my clarity. She seemed unshaken by my questions, even my doubts about God, doubts about myself, and my shakiness on the contemplative way. Her steadfast confidence and her composure helped me before she even spoke.

Her first words of response were directed to me, not to my doubts, but to the effects of my contemplation, to the things that were happening to me. She asked, "Have you not told me that you are at peace?"

"Yes."

"Well, what does that mean?

"Are not people coming to you with questions seeking guidance from you?"

"They are."

"What do you suppose draws them to you?" She continued to press me with questions: "Did you not tell me that a stranger, a hostess at a restaurant, asked if you were a minister because she felt in you a calmness of spirit? Do you think this is related to your contemplation?

"If you are asking me about living in delusion, I'd have to say that I see all these signs as God marking your journey. Don't be afraid when the path leads into a new land of liberty.

"Finally, as you review the events that brought you to this place, do you not see the invisible hand of providence orchestrating events?"

13. Correctives and Directives

I have become aware of several persistent questions, like how effective are my efforts in contemplation and how much depends upon God? How can an ordinary person find a life of contemplation? In response to this wondering, Merton offered a partial answer to my question with a description of three types of contemplation: active, masked, and infused.

Regarding active contemplation he says "this perception is attained in some measure by our own efforts though with the mysterious and invisible help of grace." This reference to "our own efforts" offered guidance in my role in the life of contemplation which I understand to be preparation and persistence. To persist on the road to contemplation requires effort on my part assisted by God's grace.

I also find further clarification of my journey in the notion of "masked contemplation," a way of deep union with God in the active life. Masked contemplation belongs to those who do their contemplation through their work. In some sense their work becomes their contemplation. This reminds me of a doctor friend of mine who practices this kind of contemplation by being absorbed in his work as an act of service to

God. Yet, he would be shocked at my labeling him a contemplative. Indeed, contemplation applies to the devout, who are neither retired nor live in monasteries.

Infused contemplation refers to those moments when God's grace embraces us in a supernatural manner and unites us with Godself. High and lofty phrases like "the life of union," "united with the triune God," or "the divine marriage" are used to describe this mystical experience.

It is not wise to make any of these types of contemplation objectives to be achieved. We are to continue on the path to God and let the various aspects of contemplation occur naturally. Realizing that at times contemplation requires our efforts, there is a contemplation that flows spontaneously. One place that contemplation may occur naturally is in the responsibilities, tasks and relationships of daily life.

I am an infant in contemplation, but growth is possible.

14. Show Me the Way

As I sat down for my silent time with God, the prayer that I needed to pray came to me: "Show me the way to contemplation." Why was I so long in making this request with my lips? I am convinced that my heart has prayed for guidance and assistance a hundred times, but since my awakening to this journey, I have never clearly stated this request. This prayer made my yearning and seeking explicit, though it had been implicit all along!

Today, when I began my silence, the prayer of the heart became the prayer of my mind, and it fell soundlessly from my lips. Almost immediately I began to relax deeply; it was as though I was taken by the hand and directed into the silence. It seemed that I was escorted into the realm of the Sacred where there were no images.

My awareness felt sharp and very focused. On other occasions I have permitted my attention to become slack, letting it sag into unconsciousness. My relaxing of attention was an effort to drop all thoughts and images and emotions in order to find unity with God, or to place myself where God could unite with me. But Merton helped me to see that contemplation does not lead to a blank mind as in Quietism, and that the exertion of effort has a role until I experience infused contemplation. Besides, if I have relaxed my awareness too deeply at 5:00 a.m., I go to sleep.

Today I looked at my watch when I began my prayer, "Show me the way to contemplation," and it was 5:55 a.m. Then my mind became keenly aware of the Presence, which remained without distraction. Both focus and clarity were gifts. Afterward, I remembered being aware throughout my silence – not asleep. And when I next looked at my watch, the time was 7:00 a.m. Strange! I had no sense of time. Stranger still, I have no memory of that hour except a focused awareness.

Am I on the road to contemplation? Is this what contemplation means?

15. On Meeting Another

In years past it has been my practice when meeting another person, especially a stranger of note, to exude extra energy to make a good impression or to engage the person or to take control of the relationship. These various responses were neither studied nor feigned – they were habit, routine and regular. I think these ways of meeting others spring from two sources: my need for attention and desire to control.

I once had honest feedback when a 'friend' said to me, "I don't want to get too close to you, lest I fall under your control and become used." I did not understand this response and for a long time I was not aware of my behavior and how it affected other people. I likely learned these various ways of encountering others through my primal role models coupled with my insecurities and my falsely perceived needs.

As a consequence of my contemplation, I am seeing more clearly my frightening and destructive modes of meeting new persons. I recognize ways that my meeting another person is beginning to change. I feel less need to impress or to take charge of the encounter. This change in the way I meet people became clearer when I met another like myself. She arrived at the house where we were visiting and she was dressed to impress. Her manner was straightforward and aggressive. Without waiting to be introduced, she said, "My name is Darlene," and then proceeded to establish herself by where she had gone to school and all the glamorous things that filled her life.

I felt somewhat shocked at how dead my ego was to the challenge. I had no desire to compete or "flash my wares," so to speak. Rather, I found my silence and remained there.

This episode reminded me of Henri Nouwen's statement when he and a couple of fellow retreatants met Thomas Merton. Nouwen said,

"He refused to play Thomas Merton for us." I pray that God will give me grace never to play Ben Johnson again. This behavior unmasks the false ego that must die.

16. Signs of Contemplation

As I walk this path of unknowing, I continue to lack certitude. My mind continues to function without a pseudo-assurance, yet I still grope for signs that I am on the right way and that I am not alone. And, from time to time, just when I desperately need confirmation it comes to me – a text, a word from one of the classics, or the affirmation of my guide.

Most recently the word came from a classic in spirituality, Merton's *Inner Experience*. He identified three signs of the beginning of infused prayer: seeking, forgetfulness, and attraction. The first steps on the way to contemplation are characterized by a persistent seeking. The seeking takes the form of prayer without feeling and searching without seeking. It does not get discouraged in the absence of consolations. For nine months I have thought of little else but this contemplative way to God. Without any great effort, I find myself getting up between 4:00 a.m. and 5:30 a.m. possessed with the thought of being present to God.

Second, the easy steps on the way occur in a kind of forgetfulness. The way becomes so compelling that simple, everyday things fall by the wayside. I don't yet see strong evidence of this descriptor, except forgetting to dress, occasionally failing to eat, and occasionally neglecting an appointment. Perhaps the greater forgetfulness is the forgetfulness of my self.

A third early characteristic of infused prayer is a strong attraction for the contemplative way. It consists in a hunger within and a magnetic drawing without. The core of one's person feels drawn to God. I feel this attraction to God. The drawing power flows from a sense of being 'called' to this way. Even stronger I feel a sense of destiny in what is happening – a God-initiated, God-sustained attraction to what I am to be.

I believe that I see minuscule evidence of these three indicators in my life today. Maybe one day there will suddenly come an awakening to a new level of experience.

17. Seeing Through A Sermon

While traveling in another state, on a Sunday morning I went to church. Because the pastor had been my student, I had a desire to hear his word. I felt disappointed. The sermon not only was trivial, superficial, and shallow, it was also disappointingly culture bound. His subject was superb: "What is the meaning of life?" He identified three futile ways to search for life's meaning: the mystical, the practical, and the philosophical.

As I listened to his easy dismissal of these three possibilities of finding the meaning of life, it became obvious to me that he had never made his own journey inward. Not even his declaration that God revealed the purpose of life in Christ could rescue the sermon. I felt no judgment for this fine young man, but I did feel a deep grief and a degree of pity. How empty will his cup become unless he finds a way to drink from the fountain bubbling up in his own psyche!

To save the worship experience from a complete loss, I turned his sermon upside down. Yes, it is true that God has revealed the meaning of life in Christ, and he provides a mirror in which I gaze at my true self, and Christ also serves as the magnet of God to draw out my true self. The mystical way by which he shows us our Self and by which he liberates us by his Spirit requires a long journey inward led by the Spirit. On this journey we continue to discern both our identity and our destiny.

The practical way, which received such disdain, actually points to preparation that provides the setting for God to speak. Most of us find that these practices of prayer, reading and silence are both educational and experimental.

The philosophical aspects of discovering life's purpose demand that we weave God's intention into the fabric of life itself. Not a bad sermon when stood on its head.

I wonder if the contemplative way causes me to look at the essence of things.

18. Steady Calm

For as long as I can remember I have experienced highs and lows. The swings in mood don't quite qualify as manic/depressive, but the changes in outlook and feelings have been frequent enough to note. My perception of my world and myself seem to be more stable and positive. Whether these changes stem from my age and growing maturity, or from less stress, or from the effect of my contemplative journey, I cannot say for sure. But I can say that I notice a change in my mood and demeanor. I consistently experience a steady calmness. In that calm place I am at ease with myself with fewer shifts in emotion.

In times past I have needed an occasional emotional high to feel alive. I searched out possibilities to get that feeling of being real, alive, and ecstatic over an idea, plan, or large expectation. One day I focused on an achievement to which I felt committed. On another day the thought of a trip, a game, or a party stimulated my expressive side. Having friends for dinner also released a sense of excitement. Feeding on these mundane events unconsciously constituted much of my life.

But there was another side to this emotional addiction that sought volcanic eruptions of pseudo-joy. The dark side, the underbelly of this soul excitement, crept into my mind as depression. My depression never reached the depths that many persons suffer with, but I had enough to ruin a perfectly good day. My depression began with a mood change, a turn toward darkness. On those days the future held no promise. I felt lifeless, and so I filled my emptiness with work. No matter what technique I used to try to lift myself out of the bubbling despair, the darkness and uncertainty remained.

This roller coaster of alternating highs and lows has begun to change. Since the vision of Christ and the Word that I heard at the mentor retreat, my emotions have been settling like silt settling to the bottom of a jug, leaving the water clear. I seem to have fewer highs and lows. When I have either, I do not pay attention whether the feelings are bright and cheery or dark and anxious. In a manner beyond my capacity to explain, I have entered into a calm stillness where all is well. And with the confidence of Julian of Norwich I, too, can say, "All is well, and all shall be well."

19. Confirmation From the Voice of a Friend

From time to time I send my writing to a trusted friend who will listen carefully and respond honestly. A while back I asked a deeply sensitive saint of God to listen to my musings on some of the ideas of Thomas Merton.

She wrote: "These words are more than musings; they are profound questions from your soul. As I read them I found myself wanting to hurry through them in a hungry sort of way. I wanted to siphon off their inspiration. Regarding the path you mention when you feel there is a new step for you to take, when something manifests itself and pulls you along, I think that you are right to name that sense of direction the manifest presence God.

"The experience of guidance and what results from it far exceeds word symbols; they cannot grasp and hold the insight or meaning, but nonetheless, we try to compel them to carry a load that their inadequate structure cannot handle. I, too, like to roll the words around in my head until I can absorb the truth lodged in them, but they are woefully inadequate for the task.

"Such a manifestation of the Divine came to me one day as I was listening to a reading of the baptism of Jesus. In the baptismal water what is, what was, and what is to be were all present to me in the moment. The insight was fleeting, and when I sought to grasp and hold on to it, it was gone. So brief! So inaccessible! And, yet so powerful! I perceived that all that is, all that was, and all that shall be poured down in the waters of baptism. God's words to Jesus conjured up God's Word to me.

"Like Merton, we all hope to restore old words worn thin by use and drained of their energy through careless unthinking lips. One of those words for me is, 'Father,' as it pertains to God. My difficulty does not arise from a poor relationship with my earthly father, but from the sense that God is beyond either Father or Mother. My problem with this dominant male image is regularly made more complex and difficult by the prayers of an elder who without exception addresses God as Father.

"Your word about restoring words to their original power applies directly to this word. Recently, when this elder prayed and as always said, 'Father,' something happened to me. I felt a physical sensation in my heart area. It caught me unaware. I stayed in the moment. Something of the Divine mystery encompassed me and something of the Father was manifest in that moment. I held that word in my mouth, rolled it around and spoke it now and again. Perhaps it is being restored to its original power and meaning. So your words are becoming God's word to me both in what you say and in what your words cause me to recall."

What more could I hope for in sharing my journey?

20. Receiving Guidance and Seeing Signs

These two issues hold great significance for anyone seriously on the spiritual journey. Thomas Merton condenses the substance of these issues for those on the path to contemplation. First, his words on guidance: Anyone on this way needs a spiritual guide lest he or she fall into confusion about the work of the Spirit and face numerous unnecessary obstacles. The beginner in contemplation needs to have an idea of what God is doing in the soul, and this comes from a wise guide, or reading, or reflecting on the personal experience of God. All previous ways of conceiving and understanding God seem no longer to work.

"If this is true, what am I to do?" you might ask. And I would answer, "Do not stir yourself. Seek peace and quiet. Retire from excessive action. Be simple in activities. Love and serve God. Remain recollected in all your work. Calm your soul and rest in the light of God. Do not seek to be spectacular. Do not be too anxious about your advancement in the ways of prayer, because you have left the beaten track and are traveling by paths that cannot be charted or measured."

I have sought to understand my experience of contemplation through the time-tested signs of the Spirit as witnessed by many who have walked the contemplative pathway. They testify to me that when a person is on the contemplative path and loses the rational knowledge of God, the rational side weakens, the intuitive gets stronger. Eventually the inability to grasp God in concepts prevails. For me this has meant prayer without an image of God. God is like God!

Further, those who write about the dark path of contemplation suggest that one does not receive much consolation on this journey. I find that I no longer look for or expect to receive God's consolation in prayer. I do not experience the joyous consolation of the Lord's presence as I once did, but I do experience an amazing calmness in my life.

These same guides like Merton and Finley suggest that the imagination is of no help in the naked encounter with God. My imagination seems to have been darkened and of no use in prayer. Images seem to take me away from God whereas once they drew me closer to God.

Perceiving God as the Supreme Reality occurs along this pathway. I am not aware of yet having had an encounter with God at the end of my contemplation. Rather than meeting Reality, I seem to be encompassed by it.

I see the signs of mute attraction and peaceful rest as signs that I am being drawn into a contemplative manner of prayer. The attraction to God is a kind of silent speech, and I think that I feel it in my quiet desire for God. My desire is not a grasping, panicked longing but a sincere quiet desire. I do receive the peace that Christ promised; it seems to pervade all my waking moments.

21. Discernment and Response

"If you possess the gift of discernment, you must take precaution not to become judgmental," said my spiritual guide. I realize that what I do with my discernment must be handled cautiously. When I see into a person or a situation, I need not always speak aloud what I see. On one occasion I may dismiss the perception altogether, while in another I may evaluate its accuracy or muse over its implications. Even when I conclude the correctness of the discernment, it must not ever be used to judge, condemn, discount or expose another person. Perhaps, if their behavior violates the truth of God's love or places a brother or sister at risk, something may need to be stated. Yet communicating an unrequested perception seldom receives a warm welcome.

These insights into living with the gift of discernment came freshly to my mind as I listened to an array of speakers at a conference. Some came from high places in our government; others spoke from more common points of view. All, I believe, had a mind to honor God and speak truth.

As the highest ranking government official spoke, his words were platitudinous and devoid of his soul and of power. Another spoke with great sincerity, but his message had worn smooth by his telling it again and again. Though filled with suggestive images and moving descriptions, it had lost its cutting edge and seemed more like a performance than a speech out of his present struggles. It was as if he were telling another's story. But his successor spoke with openness, employing living metaphors and emotional engagement. His manner intrigued me. But the high moment came when the last speaker opened his life to the assemblage. His carefully chosen words drew me into his message. Obviously, he lived in his words and with each utterance he entered deeper and deeper into my heart.

I believe the discernment of God in these speakers was accurate. I believe God used each of them for good, but what I most clearly realized was how I used my discernment for judgment, evaluation or exposure. I associate this discernment with a deepened sense of God. Perhaps the silence begets a guarded muteness around truth discerned.

22. Image and Loss of Image

I hope that each of these reflections will describe a bit of experience on the pathway into contemplation. Although each of us has a unique path to walk, surely there is a commonality of experience that we share. The ones that I share do not substitute for God and God's way with others; they are pointers drawn from one person's experience and nothing more. What I am offering to others is what I have wished for in my own quest and have only found in bits and pieces in various conversations and writings.

I hope that each of my reflections holds one new insight, a bit of guidance and encouragement for someone who is struggling and groping as I am. For example, today I began my meditation with relaxation. My breathing was slow and studied. As I listened to my breath, I felt my body quieting down. Bit by bit I began to become stilled and gradually quiet inside.

But before the stillness came psychic rumbling. I watched these emotional billows roll until their energy subsided. As they calmed down and lost their energy. I prayed in much the same way that I have for years. I said these words:

"Thank you for a night's rest and for the sight of a new day."

"Forgive me for any boundaries I overstepped yesterday."

"Bless those in my family who mean so much to me."

"I ask you to guide me on the path to contemplation."

In the immediate quiet that followed I entered into a profound stillness that bordered on the holy. For some time I was suspended in holy silence. For how long, I do not know, because in intervals like this, time disappears under the breath of eternity. In that moment of timelessness, I consciously endeavored to maintain a studied awareness – not thought nor feeling or desiring, but alertness.

Then I had a vision of a circle containing a series of smaller circles tangent to each other, a dozen or so. Then I saw an object dropped in a cauldron with a foggy mist rising from it. This strange object got lost in the mist; it was encircled by the mist and then dissolved in the mist. It disappeared. It occurred to me that the object's fusion with the vapor offered a paradigm of union with God.

In this state of awareness I kept very still. I do not know what happens between God and my soul in moments like this. I think that I was waiting alertly at the edges of contemplation.

23. Entering the Stillness

When I sit down in my favorite chair in my chosen place, entering the Great Stillness begins. Sometimes I do not use any practices to still my body and reduce the tensions; when I sit, the body seems to know. And, it knows also when I don't sit to meditate. It even knows when I neglect it altogether. Throughout the day it emits tiny signals that tell me that I have failed to engage the silence. These reminders do not carry condemnation or judgment; they remind me of my lack of focus and emptiness. This forgetfulness at the beginning of the day results in irregular recollection during the day and a dull lack of mindfulness, as well.

Today when I began to center in the stillness I said, A Praise, A Thanks, A Confession, A Petition and An Intercession for a couple of persons. Even while I was praying, something pressed me into the stillness demanding silence.

As I entered into the silence, I saw a window open into the vast expanse of a yet greater silence. The opening came like a rectangle on the computer screen when I edit a photograph or when I click on a word box and a picture appears. The window in my vision swung open revealing shadowy, vague forms, and all was dark except for a dim light that shone from the upper right hand corner of the rectangular picture frame.

From time to time I wrote a word or phrase on a sheet of notepaper, but now as I read them, I don't recall what they meant. Slowly but surely my mind and soul went deeper and deeper into the great pool of stillness. My mind rested there in the silence for the better part of an hour.

As I seek to recall the next hour, it is elusive; it is like my awareness merged into the deepest, most basic form of consciousness. I wonder, too, if I did not sink into the unconsciousness of sleep! Yet, as I recall it, the total stillness was accompanied by a keen awareness.

24. Entrusted

The things that are happening to me on the path to contemplation alternate between deep inwardness, like entering the ocean of stillness, and being entrusted with stories not often told. These hidden stories often do not find their way to our ears and illuminate our understanding because we are not prepared to hear them. But from time to time I recognize another person on the path, and I receive assurance that some persons can hear and appreciate reports of these rare moments.

A couple of friends, husband and wife, were visiting with us and the woman said, "We want to tell you what happened to us on a recent retreat. In the opening session, though I did not say it, I felt deeply troubled about Tom. He has been depressed and not himself at all."

When Tom spoke, he described how he went to the retreat with a dilemma about God's speaking to him. Though deeply religious all his life, he had never felt that God had engaged him personally, except in retrospect as he noted some providential act of God.

Ellie, his wife, continued, telling her experience. On the first night of the retreat, she had awakened from restless sleep. She turned in her twin bed to view Tom, a few feet away in his bed. As she looked, she noted that he was facing the opposite wall with his back to her. And, she then saw his mother bending over Tom. She seemed to be speaking to him and comforting him. The words that she heard were: "You are all right. Don't worry, I'll take care of you." Then, she disappeared. The fact that his mother had been dead for twenty years made this a strange experience.

Tom, the next day, told her that he had dreamed about his early life, and how people loved and helped each other. The dream progressed through his whole life, and he began to feel in his dream that he was, in fact, okay. He did not need to leave a grand legacy; he was a person of worth; and, his life had been worthwhile. He awakened with his tension and depression dissipated. He regretted awakening and wished that he could return to sleep and to the dream.

"When we shared the vision and the dream with each other," Ellie said, "both of us felt that God had spoken to us profoundly. Our lives settled into an indescribable peace."

Tom said, "I believe that God spoke to me through the dream that I am okay, and God also confirmed this word to me through Ellie's vision."

Me? I felt trusted with the story of a "God moment" that some people would have felt the story too odd to share and would have dismissed it altogether. I wonder how these friends sharing their story with me informs and shapes my contemplative journey. I recognize that it gives me a degree of discernment; it also strengthens my confidence that God desires to show us love.

25. Waiting

When living in the rush of life with revelations coming and striking events occurring, I must confess to a certain ecstasy and personal delight. But most of my days seem very different, very ordinary. In those ordinary days I wonder what to do. I guess at my priorities. Because I've had several days like that recently, I've been faced once again with the question of my engagement with the common life. The answer came in a psalm:

> I waited patiently for the Lord;
> He inclined his ear and heard my cry.
> He drew me from the desolate pit,
> And out of the miry bog,
> And set my feet upon a rock,
> Making my steps secure.
> He put a new song in my mouth,
> A song of praise to our God.
> Many will see and fear,
> And put their trust in the Lord.
> Psalm 40:1-3

As I read these words, I knew what to do – wait patiently. Waiting is not my nature; patience is not my virtue. For years I boasted that I never prayed for patience because I knew the kind of occurrences that birthed it. But I suppose that I have avoided this virtue as long as I am able.

As on other days, I had asked God to guide me on this contemplative journey, and the direction came in the psalm. Today I receive this ancient prayer as God's response. When I am not aware of what is happening in my journey, patience is my call. I am to wait and to persist in waiting with patience. In God's own time, the Spirit will draw me up, set my feet, secure my steps, and give me a new song of praise.

In the simple act of accepting my helplessness I find a peace in waiting. Later on in this ordinary day when a friend did not show for lunch at the agreed upon time, I remembered and waited quietly until he arrived. Patient waiting relates to our inward journey and outward circumstance. Yet, how well I know that one act of waiting does not a patient person make!

Brother Carlo says, "All our life is one of waiting for the God who comes."

26. Just a Glimpse

Sometimes I experience just a glimpse, a glimpse into the nature of things. Even a hasty blink has lasting significance by reminding me from time to time that the things I long for and hope for are true. The kind of glimpse to which I refer is quite different from that of a squirrel hiding behind a tree or a deer dashing across the road or a stranger disappearing around the corner. We often speak of getting a glimpse of subjects like these, but this is not the glimpse that I am referencing. Occasionally I get a glimpse of being, of how things really are. It is a way of momentarily seeing into things.

A glimpse like this came to me the other day. It was a day that I had begun to practice waiting patiently. My car was merely one in a long line of vehicles waiting for the traffic light to turn green. While I was rehearsing patience like a child praying the Lord's Prayer, uttering about every third word correctly, I caught this glimpse. As I looked at the autos, the commercial buildings on either side of the street and the various restaurants that sold everything from pizza to Thai cuisine, it happened!

I had a momentary realization that everything I was viewing had roots in the creativity of God. Women and men made in the image of God had made these automobiles and had constructed these buildings. In so doing they had drawn from the creativity of God -- God in them manifest as creativity. In the order, symmetry and beauty of what I was viewing with my eyes, I also realized the presence of God for just an instant. I caught a glimpse of the creativity and ingenuity of God that had been placed in me and in all human beings.

In the moment I felt touched by Truth; my soul rejoiced and my mind danced with delight. That sense of having seen through the solid, opaque, material world remained with me all the way to the place of my luncheon meeting.

I cannot very well capture the impact of that fleeting glimpse in words, and that is good. If these moments could be bottled, others would quit the search for their own experiences of the Mystery of Being. I think the true contemplative lives constantly in the presence of this glimpsed reality instead of momentary flashes like I have.

The moment of vision makes me want more and more to see God in all things and to live in the celebration of this Holy Mystery.

27. Distractions and Persistent Questions

Since I began to walk on this path toward contemplation, I have known more distractions than consolations. The major distractions that disrupt me are soul-shaking questions: Is this universal, mysterious God accessible to us humans? Is union a possibility or is this a height to which humans cannot reach? Why is my prayer so dry? If the way is one of "unknowing," how can I ever hope to have certitude? Is claiming that contemplation follows the way of "unknowing" a way to cover up the nothingness of the path to keep me from discovering that it eventually leads nowhere? If I, a seeker, must relinquish even the desire for union or consolation or knowing, how can I possibly make any movement toward being one with God? Am I to wait endlessly for that which I do not know? Will I know this union when it comes? I wonder if all persons on this path experience these same questions. Is there a God at the end of this path? Or, is there a God on this path with me? And how will I know God's Spirit and discern God's voice from another voice that would lead me astray?

On the far side of all these questions there must indeed be answers. Even the hope for a possible answer drives me forward. Life is a wilderness on the way to contemplation and pioneers before me have marked it with skinned bark on the trees and pointers at turns in the way, and symbols that eventually I can make out. And, occasionally I stumble upon one of their signs and choose to follow it. Occasionally, when I most need one of them, it appears.

I am sustained on this way by the call that has come to me, which began at the Monastery Retreat. And, that call has been confirmed again and again. I have been given hope and a deep settled peace. Furthermore, my life has been given a focus that unifies my vision for the future. I am being drawn to God by daily moments of insight, the faint glimpses of reality that I cannot grasp, and the subtle changes in my behavior; all give me confidence in spite of my faltering steps. And, I do not forget those odd things that happen, like people seeing something in me that I do not see, like friends baring their souls to me, and strangers asking me direction for their lives. Whether empty or full, whether consolation or desolation, I am on a way and the testimony from those up ahead assures me that I am not lost in the dark of this wilderness, but I am following a path, which at times I cannot see.

I have not the slightest intention of forsaking my calling or turning aside from this path despite my questions, doubts and fears. I don't know if I must relinquish even this resolve, but today I have it, fully knowing that it is a gift that depends upon an "Other."

After naming all my distractions that wear the masks of fear, questions, and doubt, the most amazing thing occurred. Sitting at the kitchen table, staring through the picture window onto a patio surrounded by shrubs, decorated with a fountain against a backdrop of evergreens and hanging baskets filled with blooming flowers, I had the most amazing experience.

I snapped together my old-fashioned fountain pen with which I had been confessing my distractions and intentions on paper. I closed my eyes and began to notice how calm was my soul! It was as though a powerful vacuum had siphoned off my doubts and fears. Those disturbing demonic whispers, which lay just beneath the surface, had been silenced. In their place, a warm, soft delight filled my soul. The warm glow of a heart made clean is enough; it is an unexpected and unsought-for mercy. I choose to say no more.

28. A Japanese Maple Speaks

It was a Sabbath morning on a cold rainy day in February. I had finished writing for the day when I looked through the huge picture window at a Japanese Maple. It was a pitiful sight. The Maple stood before a mossy brick wall. The V and Y shaped limbs had the remnants of last year's foliage. The small tree appeared dead and good for nothing but to be cut down and cast out of the garden.

My vision enlarged and I noted the green, lush winter pansies, the clumps of Aucuba and the green ferns. As I looked at one of the ferns beneath the Maple, the two seemed to engage in a muted conversation.

The fern spoke first: "Maple, what has happened to you? Last spring and summer your limbs were filled with green leaves like mine and you shaded all of us ferns from the summer's heat, and in the fall you were a gorgeous picture of red, green and brown. We envied you so much! Now you are stripped naked with only a few dead leaves hanging on through the cold and rain. Will you always look so forlorn?"

The little Maple bowed its head to speak. It bent low because it had so little energy and sought to conserve its strength by whispering to the inquiring fern. "Little fern, I'm more than you can see. My exterior appears to you a spectacle – ugly, useless and dead. But what you cannot see lies inside. All the juice in my limbs has settled in my roots during the winter cold, but when the spring comes, I will be transformed again before your very eyes. Little fern, you always are lush and green; be careful not to judge others that turn dark and lose their beauty for a time. What appears to be the loss of life and purpose is nothing more than a rest stop to come forth again in blazing color and beauty."

Listening in on this conversation caused me to wonder if the way of contemplation is not akin to the life of a Maple tree. And, on this Sabbath I wondered if the shrubs and trees in the yard, and the trees of the forest really do notice each other and speak their mind, even about us. I feel rather certain that they speak, and if we are alert, we may hear them.

29. Awakening to God

As inadequate as my efforts will be, I will attempt to describe it. The notion of "becoming an icon of God" or "becoming truly human" had attracted me in the writing of Willigis Jager. Once when I finished reading, I turned toward the silence to seek contemplation. No sooner had I laid the book down and closed my eyes, than my body became relaxed and still in spontaneous preparation.

At once a sweet Spirit pervaded my consciousness; it transformed my ego-consciousness into something greater. I began to see how the Eternal God realized Godself in the creation; it was his body and God lived and manifested Godself in it, in this temporal world. Every tree and stone and canyon and river reveals the Creator God. And, I too, with all of humanity, formed the body of God.

In a short afterword, Jager wrote that the aim of human existence is to be an embodiment of this God who was constantly being manifest. And, contemplation of the divine is the manner in which the human spirit becomes increasingly imbued with the divine. By becoming transparent to the divine, humans become icons of God and bespeak God's will and nature in an unselfconscious manner.

As I waited, I suddenly saw into the theodicy issue (Why is there evil?); I saw the whole world as God's body, beautiful and lively but marred by disease, war, poverty, greed and suffering – these deformities course through the whole creation and they contradicted the gracious, good, and holy God. And, I saw that God's way of dealing with this contradiction was through Incarnation. God entered bodily into the creation in Jesus of Nazareth, and faced evil in all its sinister and deceitful forms. He did not run away from evil but overcame it. God conquered the evil of the world by letting it rip his heart out on the cross.

Words make cold and powerless the vision of the cross ripping open the heart of God for the sake of the whole creation and robbing evil of any hope of conquest. Even thoughts about the vision sap it of the warm, tranquil, loving presence that communicated it. Opening my eyes and recalling the images takes something away from the moment, but even now, I sense beneath my immediate consciousness God's woundedness for the creation.

I hope that this unexpected gift is but a forecast of where this pathway leads. And, I hope that I can willingly permit "God to be God in me" so that the eye with which I see God will be the same eye with which God sees me. (Eckhart) The whole creation pulsates with the presence of a crucified God.

30. Taught by God

I have been shown in the past and the awareness becomes clearer each day that I cannot learn to contemplate, I must be taught. My efforts only frustrate the love of God who, like a mother, longs to embrace me and guide me. The One who awakened me to this journey is the only One who can show me the way.

Seeking to profit from this wisdom, I began my quiet with a simple request: "show me the way to contemplation." Immediately, in that very instance I felt myself enveloped in the Presence of God. My mind was fully alert and open to the presence. I felt a great calm in my soul that nurtured me with grace. The awareness filled me with delight out of which came a sense of oneness with God. I am woven into all things. I have a sense of being woven into the fabric of Reality. All of this seemed to take place in a cloud that engulfed me and swept away all images of individual things.

I was shown the difference in meditation and contemplation. The experience in the cloud had no images or words and it was also void of thought, yet I was in a state of sharp awareness. But the moment I began to think about a prayer for guidance or sought to deal with an obligation, I felt myself slip across a boundary, and I briefly departed the cloud in which the contemplation occurred. But I refused the distraction of thought and entered once again into the cloud of pure presence.

At the edge of this cloud I felt that I could think of God and when I dropped the thinking, there was only God. I could feel God's presence, drop the feeling and be in God. Everything came with such ease and the hour passed in a moment because I had no sense of time.

31. No Waiting

I generally read something about contemplation before I begin my time of prayer, a book or a text from the scriptures. And, I am learning to ask God's guidance into that place where spirit meets Spirit and they kiss. Today after reading I felt an eagerness to pray, like two dancing horses in my mind, held by bits and bridles, yet pawing and prancing to get going.

I sat on my excitement seeking to quiet it, but it kept oozing out beyond my control. I wanted to fetch the prayer I had written, having not yet committed it to memory:

O God, my Father,
    Take me by the hand,
    Guide me to the path,
    Place my feet on the way and
    Lead me into the place of contemplation.
In that Sacred Space,
    Consume the dross in my soul,
    Purify the thoughts and intentions in my mind,
    Illumine the eyes of my heart, and
    Fill me with Yourself that I may become an icon of your presence.

In the split second while I was considering the need of my journal to get the words correctly, a strange, jarring thought came to me. Why should I ask to be led into contemplation when the doorway stands open before me? Get up, take the restraints off your enthusiasm, relax the reins on the steeds of yearning and desire, and let them loose!

I did. And, my task was then to steady the prancing horses with a few words and gentle pats until their nervous energy subsided, and they walked with a sustained gait while I slowly rocked in the saddle. I was one with the horse of desire as I rocked with each step.

Quickly, ever so quickly, my thoughts disappeared. I recalled the difference between thinking and being that I had learned in the cloud. In that recollected moment, I lost all sense of time.

32. The Eternal Now

The joining of these two words is not new to me. I have heard the phrase since my earliest years when in my adolescence I read Thomas Kelly's A *Testament of Devotion*. Though it attracted me like a flitting bird seeking a steady perch in a bush, I had no idea what it meant.

From time to time through the years, I returned to this devotional classic and the words fascinated me with the kind of interest that a fish has in a darting lure. Like many fish I never struck the lure; I never got fully hooked. Kelly was not the only fisherman for my soul; other anglers for God also cast these words before me, but to no avail.

To shift the metaphor, I think it might have been a matter of the soil. Perhaps these words fell on the path or on stony ground and had no depth to endure the sun and wind. And, I didn't get it nor did it get me.

Though I didn't get it, my desire to capture this image exceeded my understanding. All my life, at least since I was nine, I feared death. My fear was not the process of wilting like the grass of the field, but entering into eternity. The notion of unending time – forever and forever and forever – shook my uncomprehending mind like a bush in a whirlwind, and it filled me with an anxiety I could not control. Still I did not comprehend the meaning of the Eternal Now.

A time or two I almost saw it, but today as I read, I saw. Heretofore, I had looked without seeing, had listened without hearing, and I had realized without knowing. But today I saw, I heard, I knew. All my life I have thought past, present and future, and future is forever before me like the past is forever behind me. Today I see that NOW is eternity. It is neither behind me nor before me but NOW. Eternity is not the endless unfolding of years or eons. It is NOW! Was and shall be are nothing but memories and expectations of the Eternal Now.

33. Surprised by God

I do not understand the ways of God's coming into consciousness. For example, one day with high intent I quieted my body, prayed my prayer and waited to be hosted to the "place" of contemplation. It did not matter that I quieted my body, followed my breath, and spoke my prayer word. I never got to Merton's "Palace of Nowhere."

Instead, my mind never got centered, images danced in my head and voices whispered from the edge of the path beckoning me to step aside on diverging trails. With determination I sought to silence the voices but they droned on, occasionally laughing at my faltering efforts. The nets I cast around those enticing or distracting images came back empty. Even though these self-initiated efforts cannot bring me into true contemplation, I tried anyway. Preparation is important though it holds no guarantees.

Finally, I gave up. No self-judgment or gossipy condemnation of myself! Like so many times when I have gone fishing and sat all day catching nothing, the spirit of prayer escaped me. Yet, the lack of fish on my stringer never kept me from showing up the next day with rod in hand.

There are days like this that I don't understand. Some days I show up like a laborer ready to punch the clock and eager to begin the day, and it happens! Before I can get the request for guidance out of my mouth, I am centered. My thoughts lie asleep in the light of a blue cloud and I am aware of being in the Sacred Realm, a place deeper than thought.

The contemplative spirit comes almost immediately, and even when I ask a grace for my companions, my contemplation does not cease. Persisting in the background of my mental utterances, I also feel the spirit of contemplation. Contemplation remained background to the foreground of my intercession. It was as if my consciousness functioned on two planes at once — an active intercessory plane and a receptive, contemplative plane.

When I finished the intercession in my conscious mind, the contemplative spirit again filled me (or emptied me) and the hour hastened by. Afterward, writing these words was as effortless as riding a waxed snowboard on a black diamond run. When I had finished I was surprisingly beckoned into contemplation again.

34. Airport Contemplation

The night was short. I arose early for a morning departure to Chicago. My quiet contemplation suffered neglect, trampled by the pressure of a packed schedule. I arrived early at concourse B at Gate Four. The thought occurred to me: "Why not do your contemplation at the gate area while you wait for the boarding call."

I got seated so that I could view the expanse between concourses A and B. I closed my eyes and began to relax when a quiet direction arose from inside: "Don't retreat from the world of noise and conversation and constant activity around you; perceive God in it, in all of it." Life on the runways and approaches to the gate and in the concourses themselves appeared as active as the bubbling lava in a volcano.

My eyes were opened to see a dozen small trucks pulling luggage carts, buses carting passengers between gates, yellow service trucks with caution lights flashing, a red one entered not easily identified, a half-dozen planes lined up on the runway, baggage handlers loading and unloading, families with some children crying and others remarkably quiet, agents taking care of passengers, a white Volvo dashing along the edge of the runway – all this action I saw from my seat at Gate Four. I realized at that moment all the persons in my purview were subjects of divine love. I saw them not as impersonal objects but as images of God, doing the work of God with us who were traveling.

Behind me I heard the jovial conversation of two persons who had just met – a plethora of the usual questions and trite responses. Much louder than the small talk of these newly acquainted travelers, I hear the business talk of men on cell phones. They are reporting that they are beginning their trip; one has a crisis and he's summoning cohorts from New York to Brussels and getting his work covered by an associate. And there is more talk and noise, both mingled and garbled. Now I'm seated on the plane and the fellow across the aisle speaks as though all of us in First Class want to hear about his most recent business deal.

His thoughtlessness betrays his sense of self-importance. What kind of soul must inhabit that body?

If I ever hope to be a contemplative, I must enter a world of noise and ceaseless activity with a quiet and settled spirit. (I'm sorely tempted to tell the man on the cell phone that he is contaminating the whole cabin with his loud voice, but I actually think he may be my instructor in patience and kindness for the day.)

I embraced all that I have described both at Gate Four and from my seat on the plane as the bearers of God to me today.

35. An Undisciplined Mind

There are days when my mind seems to overflow with distractions. I continue to state this problem because it keeps recurring. On some days I seem to exert a great deal of effort to contemplate, yet I encounter numerous distractions, nothing clears my mind, my focus seems exceptionally blurred. And on other days I enter the world of silence without too much difficulty.

On a day when it is difficult to find quietness within, I seem to be the same person as before. I go about my prayer in much the same way, but I never get to the Center; my mind never settles down; I cannot find that place of inner calm. I have been a follower of Christ long enough, however, not to put much stock in a distracted day. My relation to him does not depend upon a beautiful time of quiet contemplation. He is in me and I am in him through his act of exceptional love. I am united with him despite my lack of focus. Even though I know this, another side of my psyche often erupts with musings and questions that trouble me.

A small trickle of fear begins to ooze through the sidewall of my soul. As I watch it, the trickle begins to gush with doubt clothed in questions. Is this notion that I as a human being (and not a choice one in my estimate) can be joined to God real? Is it true or merely the rationalized longing of a finite soul destined to perish? Does a person like me seek God in contemplation as a protection against the terror of extinction? Or, why would a person spend a lifetime learning about God and seek to forget it at the end of life?

I do not hear these questions – not any of them. I do not quake in view of their sharp penetration into my soul. When these questions come in the aftermath of a hard day at contemplation's court, I know with everything in me that I have been called to this path, and there is no other way for me to go!

36. Pre-Contemplation

Before I even thought of the silence of contemplation, my reading for the day stopped me cold. The writer said "…contemplation is out of the question for any one who does not try to cultivate compassion for other men." I understood this undeniable truth! Christ has formed of all humans his Body on earth (not merely the baptized, but all) and division, exclusion and elitism crucify him afresh by dismembering his Body. The image of fracturing his body evokes memories of a lifetime of withdrawing.

As a child I was taught that our family was different from the neighbors. Our yard was kept better and our family made better choices about with whom we associated and how we managed our money. This distinction between families marked the beginning of my awareness of being different from others.

This distinction grew until my spiritual conversion. I realize today that I was converted away from my sins, rather than to Jesus Christ. I tended then to build a false ego defined by what I did not do – how this made me different from other Christians. I imagine that fear widened this chasm between me and others, a fear that I would fall back into my past practices.

In the early days of this new life in Christ's Body, I heard my mentors comparing themselves (and me by implication) with other Christians who lacked an adequate view of holy living, of which, of course, we were good examples. This posture put me on the right side of how to be a true Christian and placed others on the left. In my early theological training, the emphasis continued to fall on the difference between "us" and "others" and not on the community of the forgiven.

Over the years this way of viewing myself in the Body of Christ has wielded a powerful, unconscious influence on my perceptions of and reactions to other people. Naturally, this pharisaical way of seeing myself affected both the way I saw both people and situations. After all these years, I must be converted to Christ and his unconditional love. A new choice is not enough; a resolve will not work; only Christ, Christ alone can make me a new creation. I look to him.

I seek the transformation of this false self into a self that loves everyone in the Body of Christ as my brother and sister. My only hope is in the mercy of the Lord that endures forever.

37. The Spirit Searches All

In my wondering about the validity of waiting in silence before God, this statement came to me: "For the Spirit searches everything, even the depths of God." (I Cor. 2:10) It is not my spirit that searches out the depths of God but the Holy Spirit, and it is this same Spirit that seeks my depths. The Spirit knows both my depths and God's depths.

Paul wrote about the wisdom of God, which earthly rulers did not perceive, and this very wisdom we recognize because it is given to us through the Spirit that searches the depths. The manner in which Paul speaks of wisdom seems to be equivalent to his speech about mystery, the mystery of God. This identification of mystery with wisdom suggests that the Spirit reveals the mystery of God. I am awed that the Spirit that continually searches me is at the same time revealing the mystery of God.

Doubtless the Spirit selects multiple ways to give us glimpses of the divine mystery; one way is through the contemplation of God. When I enter into the realm of the sacred, it is the Spirit that invites me. As my host, the Spirit shows me what I have not thought, felt or even imagined. Miraculously and inexplicably, the One who knows my depths as well as the depths of God brings me into a relationship beyond my understanding. Through the agency of the Spirit, I am ushered into a communion with God that I cannot achieve; nevertheless it is freely given.

This communion occurs in the silent depth of the soul beyond the reach of my awareness. It often seems that I am asleep under the anesthetic of inner silence while the Spirit operates with precision. Generally, I cannot name the Spirit's action and I cannot see immediate changes, but I live confidently that a transformation of consciousness is occurring.

38. Sleeping Awareness

From time to time I have wondered if my contemplation did not conclude with my sitting for an hour in sleep. I have good reason to wonder about such when I recall evening sessions begun at 11:00

p.m. and ending at 1:30 a.m., when I gently awaken and move from my chair to my bed. But falling asleep does not always occur, yet there is something in the contemplative state akin to sleep.

How could there not be a kinship of contemplation and sleep when contemplation occurs in the 'dark night'? Does not the image of the 'dark night,' in part at least, derive from sleep? The teachers of this way speak of putting the senses to sleep and putting thoughts from our minds. This suggests to me that the rational mind and the bodily emotions are sent to bed. The dismissal of the human faculties leads to the way of 'unknowing,' which borders on sleep.

What is left in the contemplative? Awareness capable of attentiveness! In contemplation all other human faculties sleep while awareness remains awake.

One morning, this alertness became clear to me. My settling in had been a struggle. Before I began to relax, a huge question popped up in my mind, like an unwelcome pop-up on my computer. Even writing answers did not disconnect me from the question; there was no delete button or mouse to X out the distraction. As the issue subsided, I fought with other images and dreamlike narratives. Finally, like two kittens exhausted from play, both of these seemed weary from the struggle and they wandered over and lay quietly in the corner, and finally disappeared.

It seemed that only awareness remained and I became focused. I gazed at the invisible for a time. After an hour I felt finished. In the moment that followed, 'sleeping awareness' became a synonym for contemplation.

39. Transformation

I have noted an amazing transformation taking place inside me. I cannot adequately capture it with words, but a few similes point toward my experience. What I am trying to describe is the conquest of the angst of finitude, a struggle that has been near me for many years.

In years past this 'black hole' of the soul has spewed anxious fears into my consciousness with such force I have shivered like a homeless child standing naked on a street corner in freezing temperatures. Something is happening to this hole in my soul. It is like my black hole is being filled up and can no longer gape at me like a sinister spirit. Sometimes I'm not certain whether the pit is being filled or its darkness is being made luminous and rendered mysteriously unthreatening.

At times the dark bottomless pit has seemed covered with a floor, which kept one from being drawn into it and falling forever. I have felt in constant danger because the protective covering had rotted and just one false step would be disastrous. If this is the right analogy, the covering has been repaired.

On other occasions this inner state has seemed like a cage of vicious, wild animals, at once all growling and squawking and chewing at the wire cage. At any moment I feared that they would get loose and consume me. Now all these threatening creatures seem to have been tamed. They are all lying down at rest.

For some reason these fearful feelings from the shadowland of the soul have appeared, but they have had no power to disrupt the sense of peace and wholeness that has begun to pervade my inner being. The result has been no more than a dud firecracker that barely made a sound when it exploded or a sparkler that fizzled. This experience that I am trying to describe suggests an inner transformation that is not under my control, but nevertheless real, very real.

40. What is Transformed?

After writing about the inner transformation, a couple of questions came to me: what do the images of a black hole, a bottomless pit and caged animals refer to? Do these metaphors refer to one inner state or more?

I wonder if the caged animals do not refer to the shadow side of my personality. Before I began to face my imaginations and compulsions, it often wreaked havoc in my mind, driving me to do or say things in ways and at times that embarrassed me. Are these repressed desires beginning to decrease and has being open to the manifestation of God in the dark side actually begun to clear up the Shadow? The taming of the wild beast within occurs when the Eternal Light shines into my personal darkness enabling me to make friends with this terror within.

I have also wondered if the inner conflict that generates such deep fear does not arise from the ego's contradiction of the self. Without question I have suffered from an ill-formed ego. Perhaps in my earliest years I absorbed my mother's images and expectations of me that lacked a footing in reality. In times of stress or at odd moments when the shock of not being shattered my covering, it also unleashed the disorienting fear that I experienced both as a child and as an adult.

Does the bottomless pit symbolize finitude? My finitude is constantly confronted by eternity, before which I stand helpless. To be human is to be finite and without the power in oneself to stand up to death.

As I reflect on these three lifelong issues of my soul, they seem to converge, and I am left facing my self with all its contradictions and its helplessness under the hot breath of Eternity's winds. Yet, despite my vulnerability, I am being healed by God's transforming presence. I know that it is not through my own efforts that change is occurring, but a grace is being given to me that I neither earn nor control. Should this not be true for all of us as we move closer to the final chapter of our lives?

41. The Eternal Now Revisited

Sometimes when I begin my contemplation, I still do not know how to get started. In my hesitancy I wonder where the silence will take me on a particular day. The day that I am recalling was no different. I was floundering around wondering how to be in the Divine Presence when I remember a sentence I had read in Merton: we enter into God through our true self. The self that we are in the creative mind of God provides the entryway into contemplation.

I then realized that one of the most truly human aspects of my being is my awareness – self-awareness, self-conscious being. And, I began to focus on being in awareness. Being in awareness! Simultaneously, the notion of time intruded into my awareness of being. "I am aware NOW in this existential moment."

Heretofore I had always thought of the Eternal Now as a succession of moments – one after another coming into being. So I was aware of NOW as a continuous succession of moments. But today I saw NOW not as a succession of moments but as a constant, a whole that lay beneath my changing vision of moments.

I do not know if I engaged that NOW or recognized it or was embraced by it! But I do believe that I was touched by the Eternal in that sacred moment. The Eternal Now is always present and always giving stability to my Reality; it is that infinite Mystery that penetrates all things.

In the Eternal Present all is well and all shall be well!

Contemplative Texts

1
God in Everything
All things came into being through him.
John 1:3

Contemplation finds its roots in the concreteness of the created world. The Creation invites contemplation because it bears the fingerprints of the Logos, Jesus Christ. He has shaped everything, whether trees and shrubs or stones and soil – every piece of creation emanated through the Logos like silt flows through a sieve. Flowing through him left the mark of the divine on the whole creation. And, the Creation is good!

I look on the new leaves on the maple tree and I see life -- new life – a new creation out of deadness. I gaze at a moon full and golden and I am awed. And these creations seem to be as nothing compared with a human being who bears the image of God – mind, sensibility, will and imagination.

So, there is no lack of 'created things' to lead us into contemplation. Every day presents the Created Order in a different light and when we observe it with mindfulness, we likely will see him through the material world. Yesterday I saw him in the helpfulness of a young woman at the airport security check. Her kind can be seen in dozens of places throughout the day. If I notice what is going on around me today, perhaps I will see him in something else like a struggle over a personal call or the healing of abuse.

Today, be alert to the divine reflection in the world around you.

2

Light in Darkness

*The light shines in the darkness and
the darkness does not extinguish it.*

John 1:5

Contemplation leads into the experience of pure light. This light originates in the Logos, the one begotten of the Father. And because all things came into being through him, the light rubbed off on everything so that all creation reflects the Light. This Light cannot be extinguished by either the darkness of the world or the darkness of my own beclouded soul.

Quakers regularly refer to this imparted light as the "Inner Light" or "that of God within every soul." No matter how deeply shadowed the soul may be, the Light keeps shining.

Light cannot be seen, but it makes everything else visible. I see who I am by the shining of the Light in my soul. The next step on my path appears because the Light shines ahead of me so that I can see. When I find myself in confusion and all my life seems to be chaotic, quiet waiting allows the curtains to be pulled and the true Light to shine.

Amazingly, as I make friends with the Light, I become Light. All of us are meant to be Children of the Light. As we are filled with the Light, it shines through us into the world as life and love.

Contemplate the Light until it shines upon you in its lustrous brightness and through you in its compassionate love.

3

Action

*My food is to do the will of him who sent me
and to complete his work.*

John 4:34

If contemplation does not burst the locks on the cells where monks sleep and oratories where they pray and monasteries where they live, it cannot be biblical contemplation. Jesus himself declared that his food came from doing the will of God. Those forty days of prayer in the desert and the lonely nights of prayer in the mountains and the early mornings of meeting with the Father formed but one aspect of contemplation. The other aspect centered on doing the will of God, completing the divine work in the world.

We do not walk the contemplative path for the solitary reason of preparation to do the work of God in the world; we walk this path to receive the fullness of God. Yet we cannot receive the fullness of God and remain detached from God's mission on earth. Action itself is food, doing God's will is food; and doing has its own integrity as a dimension of contemplation. "Inasmuch as you did it unto one of the least of these, my brothers and sisters, you did it unto me!"

Brother Carlo Carretto speaks of this hidden food as "contemplation in the streets." Mother Teresa knew this active contemplation as she served the poor and dying in the darkest hovels of Calcutta. This uncloistered contemplation enfleshes the will of God and saves us from Gnostic self-preoccupation. For the thousands that do their contemplation in the cell or oratory or hermitage, there must be hundreds of thousands who can only be contemplatives in the streets and offices and homes.

Therefore, act your contemplation and contemplate your actions!

4

Seeing and Doing

I tell you, the Son can do nothing on his own,
but only what he sees the Father doing;
for whatever the Father does, the Son does likewise.
John 5:19

Jesus' life and ministry, like our own, was a participation in the purpose of God. Jesus did what he saw the Father doing. His was an awakened heart and his were enlightened eyes, eyes that kept seeing the Father at work in the world. These enlightened eyes saw the Father calling Israel to repentance in John the Baptizer; these eyes saw the Spirit alive in a dozen followers; and these eyes saw God drawing a lonely woman to faith and hope when she came to Jacob's Well to draw water.

The eyes to see God at work in the world are eyes that have been opened by the Spirit. These Spirit-opened eyes see God in those who do good in the world despite their label; these eyes see God in the responses of souls seeking meaning and direction in life; these eyes see God in the lives of those who have been broken apart by life's testing; these eyes have seen mercy extended time and time again in Christian, Muslim, and Jew.

The contemplation of the presence of God in the loneliness, pain and hopelessness of sufferers draws the contemplative into their despair. The magnetism of the Spirit pulls the contemplative into action, the action of compassionate love. Contemplatives live more deeply in the world because they can see more deeply into the world and can join God in what God is doing to relieve the hurt and pain in God's Children.

In your contemplation in the street, look for evidence of the Presence of God in the world and join in God's work.

5
Life in the Spirit
For just as the Father has life in himself,
so he has granted the Son to have life in himself.
John 5:26

The Son of Man has life in himself; he shares in the life of God because God begot him. The Divine Son actually shares in the Life of the Father because he is in union with the Father. To sever this everlasting union would be unthinkable. As the Son has been given life in himself, life that sustains him, he never abuses it by acting independently. He remains with the Father always.

We humans have been made a littler lower than God (Psalm 10) -- the life and the Light of God have been placed in us. Though despoiled by "fallenness" the Son, nevertheless, came to us, awakening us and freshly imparting the Divine to us.

In contemplation our deeper self, which is the image of God, opens to the Spirit of God who unites with our human spirit. As the Father and the Son are one, we humans, too, are made one with God and the Son through the Spirit. By the mercy and love of God, we experience in our own spirit union with God.

Believe that God is in us as life and light! Open to the Light. Open to the Life!

6
Bread

I am the bread of life ...
John 6:35

For every Christian, Christ is the mediator of Life. Who is this Mediator? He is the only begotten of God; he is eternally begotten through the Spirit. This eternal begetting constitutes the ground of the Mystery of the Holy Trinity. The Eternal Son became flesh and metaphorically his flesh became food – the Bread of Life. In his life and ministry he becomes Bread for the World, and in his glorious resurrection he makes this bread accessible to all. He rises above one place so that he may be in all places. This is the meaning of the Ascension.

Jesus, under the metaphor of Bread, gives us life when we receive him. He awakens and enlivens our true selves. In him our true identity as "child of God" finds its origin and empowerment. When we confess our sins, he is the Bread of forgiveness. When we meditate on him, he becomes the Eucharistic Bread of presence. And, when I contemplate this Eucharistic Bread, he is the Bread of Union. As ground wheat he becomes bread, and communion bread becomes flesh in contemplation. In contemplation he pervades the life of the soul.

Christ is the subject of Christian contemplation and through him we become one bread, which is the Bread of Life and Bread for the World

Dare to become nourishment for the hungry of the world.

7

Flesh and Blood

Those who eat my flesh and drink my blood
abide in me and I in them.

John 6:56

The pagans of the first century labeled Christians cannibals and scorned them for their secret gatherings to practice their communion rituals. No wonder! If you take the statements of Jesus literally, the critics had it right.

But the accusers failed to grasp the symbolic and metaphorical significance of eating flesh and drinking blood. When Jesus sat at the final meal with his followers, he took bread and wine and proclaimed them his body and blood. Since that repast, Jesus' followers have eaten his flesh and drunk his blood in three ways.

Symbolically, the Eucharist of bread and wine has been to millions of persons his body and his blood.

Metaphorically, believers have partaken of his body and blood through meditation on his life and passion.

Contemplatively, when we encounter Christ in our depths, spiritually we partake of his body and blood.

In these three events we eat the flesh and drink the blood of the Son of Man.

By eating and drinking both eucharistically and metaphorically we abide in him and he abides in us.

To abide in him is like a fetus resting in a mother's womb. The fetus has her own vital organs, but it is her mother's blood that comes through her tiny developing veins. By receiving her mother's food and drink, she draws her life from the mother. She abides in her mother and her mother abides in her. She abides not by demanding or earning, but by receiving graciously and freely.

The birthing of the true self occurs when we abide in the first begotten who begets the whole family of God!

Today, abide in him!

8

From the Heart

Out of the believer's heart shall flow rivers of living water.
John 7:38

The contemplation of Jesus manifests a dual flow – inward and outward. The metaphorical life-giving water flows out of the believer's heart to make fruitful the barren desert of the world. The water originates in the heart, the center of Christ, and flows into the world through the passions of the believer.

The passions of the heart are summed up in the virtues of faith, hope and love -- faith that trusts resolutely in God; hope that creates a longed for future; and love pours out compassion along the way. These virtues constitute the water that gushes forth and makes the desert bear fruit.

Some days the water springs up in the heart like an artesian well. On other days the water is nothing more than a rivulet under gravity's pull finding the least resistant path downhill. When the water fails to flow, through tiresome work it must be drawn by a windlass and poured out on parched ground.

Contemplation stills the heart so that it fills with water. As faith deepens, the heart overflows with confidence. Hope blooms eternal and compassion finds ailing souls to heal. When contemplation fills our hearts with love, our eyes can see the despair of a man who has been jobless for a year. When a child wallows in guilt and self-hatred, hope generates a new day. Even in the darkest of night, by faith we trudge on to the dawn of a new day.

Learn to live from the heart!

9

The Light

I am the light of the world.

John 8:12

Jesus lights up the world! A stupendous claim! Light means purpose, beauty and direction. In the beginning when all things came into being through him, his presence was hidden in Creation. When he came into the world he shined upon what he had made so that more easily we could see its order, beauty and purpose.

The seminal characteristic of light is that it makes sight possible. We cannot see light; we see what light reveals. But when we walk in his light, we see the world from the radiance of his light – the order, beauty and purpose that daily unfolds about us. So, we can jubilantly exclaim with the Psalmist: "In his light we see light."

Because he is the light, he claims the focus of our contemplation. Our eyes turn within to "see" the light in our hearts and with enlightened eyes, we look at the light without to behold the world in its proper proportions

Indeed, the contemplative task invites us to gaze into the Light that we cannot see but a Light that informs and shapes everything we do see!

Look to the Light until you become light!

10
The Gate
I am the Gate.
John 10:9

Ask him the question; he will answer you with truth.
What do you wish from contemplatives; what role do they serve?
I am the Gate – the way by which you enter and by which you also
    exit.
Without me you cannot find your way in and out.
Without me you dare not go out.
I am the Gate into silence
I am the pathway to your true self.
I am the opening of the Mystery.
I am the presence and guide in darkness.
By me you enter the deep silence that leads to the self I intended,
the Mystery that allures you and
the darkness that often hides the pathway.
Entering the Gate --
Pursuing the course --
Following to the end –
    All take courage and hope.
At the end of your seeking
    the gate appears.
When you cannot find your way,
the gate opens before you.
Walk through, my friend, and
    I will walk the way with you!

Watch for the Gate to open before you.

11

Get Understanding

Understand that I am in the Father and the Father is in me.
John 10:38

Union is possible! Even though it may never ever happen to me, it has already occurred in Jesus and it has happened to other humans; at least, they say it has. Jesus made every effort to help his contemporaries realize that he was living the divine life in history; he was the supreme manifestation of the Holy God.

When he met resistance, he appealed to their authority, the Law. "Does it not say that you are gods?" If the law affirms humans as divine, whatever that means, does it not at least mean that God is in them as God was in Jesus?

Jesus also appealed to the authority of his works – look at my deeds and understand that they come from God. He healed. He fed. He forgave sins. Is this not godlike? What does it imply when these works occur through a believer?

Jesus' words, "I am in the Father and the Father is in me," suggest a climax in the unfolding of sacred history, a union of the divine with the human, a union of God and man. Since the dawn of creation, God has come closer and closer to humans: first God came to a people, then God came in the law, and finally God came in the flesh. In the era of the Spirit, God comes to live in a people, the church, and in each baptized believer, in you and in me. Contemplation offers a way of realizing this Eternal Incarnational Intention.

Let God be God in you.

12
Believe and See

Whoever believes in me believes not in me but in him who sent me.
And whoever sees me sees him who sent me.

John 12:44-45

In the depth of contemplation the person of Christ fades from sight and even from conscious believing. This dimming of the vision of Christ makes possible a way of union with the invisible. Yet Jesus declares that to believe in him is to believe in God, and to see him is to see God. If on the natural plane, he leads us to God, does he not do the same on the spiritual plane? Jesus leads us to God whether in the act of faith or the practice of meditation.

Today when I asked him to set my feet on the path and to lead me to the place of contemplation, he led me into the mystery where sight and believing counted for nothing. In the realm of the Sacred, words and images held no power! As they slipped away, I experienced moments of oneness with God. If we follow Christ, he will lead us into the place of holiness where we are embraced by the wonder of God and words, images, and the exercise of will drop away.

Fear not! In your blindness you will see and in your emptiness you will be filled!

13

The Way

I am the way, the truth and the life.
John 14:6

Yes, it is fact. "I am the way, the truth and the life." My child, for too many years these words have been received as exclusive, closing out some of my friends while only selecting a few others. I spoke these words as inclusive of all who find the way, believe the truth and experience the life.

Way, Truth, and Life appear most clearly to those who know my Name and deliberately follow me. On the other hand, these words do not exclude those who do not know my name. My kin according to the flesh came to the father before Way was manifest in me.

Those who know my Abba as Allah come to God and to the extent that they find the Way, know the Truth, and live the Life; it is through me whether they know my name or not.

In your contemplation sink deeply enough to find this unity of all things in me! All who find the Way, the Truth, and the Life make this discovery through me.

Find the way; Seek the Truth; Live the Life!

14

The Eternal Unity

Believe me that I am in the Father and the Father is in me.
John 14:11

The Son's being in the Father is like the bird being in the air or the fish being in the sea. As the air fills the lungs of the bird and the water fills the gills of the fish, so the Father fills the Son. The Father and the Son are like the fetus in the mother and the mother in the fetus. In one sense they are two but in another they are one.

From all eternity the Son is begotten of the Father; he has always been Son, the Eternal Son. In the days of his flesh the Christ remained in the Father and the Father continued in his Son. Even now the Son has taken into that relationship the earthly experience of humanness – limits, pain, vulnerability. In the incarnation he not only brought God to us, he ascended and took us into God.

Indeed, this initial participation is hidden in the mystery of God. We cannot understand this mystery, but we can contemplate it and thereby enter into it. By virtue of his incarnation and ascension we are in the Son and he is in us as we are in God.

Let yourself become as intimate with Christ as Christ is with God!

15

Another Advocate

…I will send you another advocate … who will be with you forever.
He abides with you and shall be in you.

John 14:16-17

The other Advocate, which is the Holy Spirit, who has come as a gift from the ascended Christ and is the Spirit of Christ, will be present in us forever. In his resurrected humanity Christ is now in the Father; in his Spirit he also abides in our humanity. In both instances we have one who is our Advocate with the Father.

In us the Spirit advocates against our temptations and weaknesses. When doubts arise, Spirit slays them with the sword. When failures and sin leave us with doubt and fear, Spirit assures us that God accepts the broken and the Spirit leads us through our darkness into the light of contemplation.

In our contemplation of Christ we realize that our fallen humanness has been glorified in the presence of God. In God's presence the Son ever lives to make intercession for us and thus to liberate us to live fully human lives with joy and confidence.

Expect him in every temptation and failure!

16

Dwelling in Indwelling

Do you not believe that I am in the Father
and the Father is in me?

John 14:10

An astounding mutual indwelling! Christ in the Father, the Father in Christ and Christ in me. Clearly he speaks of the divine/human union and Christ stands at the center as the Mediator. (The one who stands between, in the middle, the mediator between God and humans). The holy God on the one side, human beings on the other, and Christ, the God-Man joining both to each other.

When we meditate on this mystery, our minds hit a wall in short order; our reason cannot take us very far. Our minds cannot grasp the truth of this mystery. We may seek to grasp it, walk around it, view it, wonder about its profundity, and yet we feel helpless to comprehend it. Our efforts to realize the Mystery in which we live continually staggers our imagination, which remains helpless to comprehend this Mystery.

Contemplation may be of some assistance; it takes the way of 'unknowing.' What the powers of human reason stumble over, the human spirit realizes. Bowing before the mystery of God in Christ and Christ in me does not yield understanding but transformation. Being present to the mystery, of which I am a part in an inexplicable way, makes me vulnerable to the Holy and consequently change inevitably occurs.

Occasionally, after being encircled and wrapped in the Mystery, I seem to smell the perfume of the divine presence. And, sometimes I recognize that the thoughts and feelings that have arisen in me originate from the incomprehensible fact that he is in me and I am in him.

Seek continuously to notice the indwelling!

17

God at Home in Us

"We will come into her (him) and make our home in her (him)."
John 14:23

How utterly amazing that God in Christ, like a robin nesting in a tree, would be pleased to make a home in me. The Advent hymn proclaims this truth – "Pleased as man with men to dwell, O come, O come Emmanuel." God builds and furnishes a home in humans much like the bird builds a nest -- one stick at a time, one twig at a time, one feather at a time.

God's persistent coming into us extends beyond a casual visit. The dwelling place of God must be more than a beach house visited occasionally to escape the summer heat. To house God in us not only means that God is intentional and regular, but diligent, and unrelenting too. No longer a guest, God in Christ becomes a permanent resident. Even before God takes up full-time residence in us, God dwells within us while the nesting place is being constructed.

Sometimes, in sacred moments I get fleeting glimpses of the effect of the Presence within – like a sudden realization that all the people on the escalator and I are of the same family; like I am part of the rays of the sun and the growth of the tree; or the perception of an invisible hand reaching out in the silence and drawing me into a new level of union with my permanent Guest!

Can I learn to be at home in God as God is at home in me?

Never become weary welcoming your guest.

18

The Teacher

"...The Holy Spirit...will teach you all things."
John 14:26

All of the contemplatives agree on one thing: technique avails nothing in the pursuit of union with God. What we seek, what we long for already has been given to us. Often the gift comes to us through the instruction of the Spirit, who like a faithful guide, takes our hand and leads us down the path.

The Spirit teaches us all things and the teaching is personal, immediate and transformative. The Spirit's instruction begins when we have exhausted the techniques of relaxation, the repetitive word spoken silently, or the act of centering and re-centering our attention. In that moment when we have exhausted our efforts and we do not know the next step to take, the Spirit speaks. So often the Spirit directs in gentle thoughts and leads us beyond words or ideas or feelings to the place where it is no longer "I and Thou," but I in Thou and Thou in me.

We realize this momentary union with a hasty glance, a passing image that we catch in our peripheral vision. What we long for seldom comes directly like beholding our face in a mirror.

Let us learn to attend more closely the subtle lessons of the Teacher!

19

Peace

"My peace I give to you."
John 14:27

Peace, the bequest of Jesus Christ to the world. Strange how the Prince of Peace has stirred such unrest, confusion, conflict and war in the world on the one hand, and abiding peace and calm on the other. What is the relationship between these two contrasting consequences of his coming?

Contemplation enables the seeking soul to find a peace that permeates the restless spirit and unifies the conflicted soul. Could it be that peace in the world demands peace in the soul? Can the divided heart ever know an abiding peace? If individuals cannot find peace, how can the world ever hope to discover it?

The relinquishment of false attachments, the purification of conflicting drives and the surrender of selfish goals open the door to peace. When, and only when, we are at peace with ourselves can we be at peace with our neighbor and a bearer of peace in the world.

Stop! Claim your peace in every unfolding moment.

20
Unity

"I am the vine, you are the branches."
John 15:5

Meditation leads to contemplation. On this pathway one turns a corner only to discover that the efforts to muse over gospel images or beloved truths yield little help for the soul. In meditation we read the text, "I am the vine and you are the branches" and we turn the words over in our minds. We reflect quietly and wait for images to arise in our minds and insights to grasp our reason, and then we pray. We bring the fruit of our meditation into our communion with God. Our meditation reveals to us that the Vine precedes the branch, the branch depends on the vine for sustenance and a sense of connectedness. Life in the vine flows into the branches.

But our imagination moves beyond the specifics of the various aspects of the interrelatedness of vine and branch. There comes a time that the imagination seems paralyzed. No images appear; no succor comes; and our search yields nothing. This dryness of soul signals the emergence of a new way of realizing God in us. Perhaps, it is the transition into contemplation.

In contemplation the vine and branch is realized in its wholeness, not in separate images but together as a lump. It is held together as a lump to be dissolved in the soul. The soul moves beyond all images and thoughts to engage directly the Reality toward which "vine and branch" can only point. And, in this holy event, even though it is momentary, the unity of the Vine and the branch is realized. Meditation brings us into unity with Christ through the separate functions of the soul, and contemplation leads into an undifferentiated wholeness of union with Christ.

Let the life of the Vine flow into the branch!

Attend to the opportunities to become more deeply grafted into Christ.

21
Abiding
"Abide in me as I abide in you."
John 15:4

To abide means to live in, to remain with the bounds of or to last for a period of time. Where do you abide? Is your house your dwelling place? You may depart but I will remain; I will stay where I am. And, my truth will abide forever, that is, continue into the future. All these insights are valid and yet they evoke different images of abiding. There is another way to grasp the great truth of abiding.

On the spiritual journey you abide in Christ by living your life in and through him. We could say with the Psalmist, "I keep the LORD always before me; because he is at my right hand, I shall not be moved. Therefore my heart is glad, and my soul rejoices; my body also rests secure." (Ps. 16:8-9)

In another sense, the person abiding in Christ plays within certain bounds. Like the basketball player must stay within the lines to retain possession of the ball, the soul on a spiritual path walks within the bounds of love.

To abide in Christ means to take a direction for a period of time, for the full making of the journey. In a person abandoned to Christ every step is a step on the pathway and a move closer to union with Christ.

We abide in Christ both through meditation and contemplation. In meditation the truth of Christ is like a lozenge dissolving on the tongue, and contemplation resembles swallowing the truth whole. Once swallowed, the truth of Christ dissolves in the soul and filters through the whole person. By osmosis the abiding Christ disperses himself through all the spiritual faculties of the soul. At some point the believer can say with St. Paul, "I have been crucified with Christ; and it is no longer I who live, but it is Christ who lives in me." (Gal. 2:19-20)

Take the truth whole and it will wholly take you!

Repeat the text, "Abide in me and I in you," and swallow what you can.

22

Chosen

"You did not choose me but I chose you..."
John 15:16

To choose requires a decisive act – awareness, persuasion, and decision. To be chosen requires nothing of me. I do not choose to be chosen because the choice is that of another; his choice of us shows us our worth or desirability or usefulness. Since he has chosen us, we can recognize it, revel in it and trust in the power and rightness of the divine choice.

God's choice of us provides the foundation of our call to the path of contemplation. Because we have been chosen, God calls us, and this call to attend to his presence and will is continuous. God is always calling! When the sound of his voice awakens the sleeping Christ within us, the first step on the pathway to contemplation has been taken.

The soul in search of contemplation may often feel forsaken, struggle to see in the darkness or yearn for greater clarity about what this Way means. In these moments of struggle the awareness that we have been chosen by God sustains us on this journey. We persist because God continues to call. We endure because God sustains us.

I desire to remember that when I walk the way of contemplation, I am always moving in the sphere of 'chosen-ness.' Nothing that I have done has gained this relationship; I am a humble recipient. When I realize my role as a recipient, I then recognize the graciousness of God's call and the marvel of being drawn closer to the one that I love. The intimacy inherent in God's choice of me becomes an experienced realization in the silence of attending the movement of God in my soul, but it only occurs when I accept this profound decision of God for me.

The chosen-ness of God leads into the Eternal Purpose of God who never chooses randomly or with fickle intent.

Let the unfathomable grace of God's choice of you drive all your choices!

23
Still He Speaks
"I still have many things to say to you..."
John 16:12

The Christ who spoke to anxious disciples by the sea still speaks to anxious waiting souls today. He spoke to them throughout his earthly ministry – parables, actions, explanations, warnings, and promises. In the final days of his life he still had many things he had not told them. Even after his death, he still had many things to say to his followers, so he sent to them his Spirit.

The entire Acts of the Apostles provides a litany of the Spirit speaking for Christ, directing the early Church, guiding witnesses to the proper place and the intended person. This short history of the early days of the Church offers illustrations of more than three hundred times that the Spirit spoke, acted or led. These instances are background to make one strong affirmation.

Still he speaks! I make this claim because I believe that he speaks to me. I have lived a lifetime listening for and responding to this voice. I most often hear his voice after a period of quiet contemplation. Contemplation clears my mind, stills my spirit and creates receptivity within me. I seem to hear him best when I do not struggle to listen. Perhaps, when I am least expecting it, the Lord is most likely to speak through the Spirit. It is almost like I hear without listening.

One Sabbath morning in a land far away, I felt that small shift in my contemplation. At that moment the pain and struggle of a sister came to mind. And then he spoke through a gentle flow of thoughts that I was to pass on to others. He speaks still, not only about us, but also about others.

Think of every experience of the day as an opportunity to hear him speak!

24

The Unfailing Guide

"The Spirit will guide you into all truth."
John 16:13

The Holy Spirit is the Spirit of Christ, and gives us in our consciousness a sense of the presence of Christ. The Spirit completes the word of Christ who had many things to say to us, things we at first are unable to hear. The Spirit guides us into truth that Christ did not speak when he was in the flesh. This guidance is particularly evident in his speaking to us in the context of our struggles today.

Christ did not speak about wordless prayer but when words fail us, the Spirit leads us into an unspeakable intimacy with God. Though Christ experienced the "darkness" on the cross, he never spoke about the dark night of the soul. In the darkness, the Spirit guides us into the light of God's presence.

But Christ did speak of losing oneself to find oneself, but it is the Spirit who leads us step by step in renunciation and realization. Christ taught that he would be in us and we would be in him, but the reality of mutual abiding only occurs through the Spirit's guidance.

The desire of Christ to guide us in our times of perplexity has been revealed to us in the early disciples' walk to Emmaus on the first Easter afternoon. Jesus joined two of his disciples who were walking to Emmaus. He spoke with them, questioned them, and responded to their inquiries before they reached their destination. All along the way, he was with them, conversing with them, but they did not recognize him. What a metaphor for us! He joins us, walks with us, and speaks with us about the things that are happening, and we do not know who he is. Then in some "breaking bread moment" our eyes are opened and we realize that he is with us.

Therefore on the way to contemplation pay attention to the impulses of the Spirit – the unexpected thoughts, the small directives, the slight yearnings, the inner confirmations – because these are the subtle forms of the Spirit's guidance into the things that Christ has yet to speak to us. In these delicate ways he still speaks to us.

Notice the signals given to you by your experienced Guide!

25
The Spirit's Aim
"He will glorify me."
John 16:14

Ever so close is the Spirit bound to the Christ. The era of the Spirit is nothing less than a continuous Advent. He glorifies Christ by showing us Christ's presence, his acts, and his character. Contemplation is the posture of receptivity to this constant flow of Christ's communication to his brothers and sisters. Among the last words that Jesus spoken on this earth were:

"I still have many things to say to you, but you cannot bear them now. When the Spirit of truth comes, he will guide you into all the truth; for he will not speak on his own, but will speak whatever he hears, and he will declare to you the things that are to come. He will glorify me, because he will take what is mine and declare it to you. All that the Father has is mine. For this reason I said that he will take what is mine and declare it to you." (John 16:12-15)

How does the Spirit glorify Christ? By guiding us into the truth about ourselves and our lives, by declaring things that are to come, by showing us the full meaning of Christ and his will for us, and delving into the infinite depth of God and declaring it to us.

While I wait in the naked silence, the constant calming of my spirit occurs when the Spirit shows me the peace of Christ. When I weary with the difficult times of prayer, the encouragement that the Spirit gives helps me determine to go on. The Spirit shows me the love of Christ in a friend who seeks fellowship. The Spirit gives me insight into the Body of Christ, after I have been in the luminous presence of the Risen One. In all of these and other ways also, Christ is honored by the Spirit revealing to us the Way of Christ.

As you enter into and return from contemplation expect the "showings"!

26

Descent and Assent

"I came from the father...I am ... going to the Father."
John 16:28

Jesus came from God. He is the flesh and blood word spoken by God to the world. He returns to that Eternal Intimacy with the Father, but he leaves the resounding echo of the Father's speech behind.

St. Paul describes the descent as a choice by Christ. Even though he was in the form of God, he did not count this equality with God a possession to be grasped and held. Rather, he emptied himself, taking the form of a servant. As a truly human being, Jesus, the servant, surrendered himself to the cross and to death. At the lowest point, the Father exalted him and gave him a name above every name. (Phil. 2:1-11) This self-emptying act of Jesus left us with an unfading vision of God who descended from the heights to explore the depths of human pain so in his resurrection he might lift us to God.

Contemplate this descent and ascent movement of Jesus – he came down that he might go up. Jesus emptied himself of divine prerogatives that he might take on human peril and pain. The movement of the human spirit is just the opposite. In prayer our spirits ascend to the Father and they descend into the world to permeate every aspect of life.

When we live in harmony with God, the echo of the Son still reverberates in and through us. Beyond this life, when we make the final ascent, we will join all the saints in celebration. Until then our contemplation is one of continuous ascending to God and descending more deeply into Self and into Life. The contemplative life is one of ascending and descending in rhythm with the Risen and Living Christ. When we enter this rhythm of the Spirit, our lives flow naturally with the intention of God.

Relax into the rhythm and permit the wave of the Spirit to lift and lower you!

27

Ultimate Oneness

"As you, Father, are in me and I am in you, may they also be in us ..."
John 17:21

Jesus prayed this prayer at the end of his ministry when he was facing death on the cross. He recalled those who had become his companions and who would continue his life and ministry on earth. For these he prayed that they might be drawn into the divine unity of the Father and the Son.

This request rises to the apex of what biblical interpreters through the ages have called "The High Priestly Prayer." In the Holy of Holies, the Great High Priest requests the Ultimate unity of all who believe in him. He prays that they may be in him as he is in the Father and the Father is in him. This prayer has included all baptized from Pentecost to the present moment. Since the followers of Christ have been unable to find this unity through logic or reason or polity or theology, perhaps contemplation offers the one untried route to unity.

Perhaps the attempt to swallow the whole lump of division and diversity would place within us a genuine love and unfailing trust of those whose language, lifestyle, worship and aim sharply contrast with our own. If we could but see them in Christ, in God, and in ourselves, maybe our fear-erected barriers would melt and the unity to which we are destined could appear. Imagine! Christ in the Father. The Father in Christ and all God's offspring joined to one another in the Father through the Son!

In the midst of increasing diversity affirm your unity with God and others.

28

Clinging

"Do not hold on to me because I have not yet ascended to the Father."
John 20:17

Contemplation leads us beyond all clinging and stands against every effort to cling to Christ. Clinging to Christ manifests our effort to grasp Christ, draw him to our self and control his presence. Whenever he comes to us, our natural desire is to cling to the wonderful sense of his presence, but to do so would put us in charge of the relationship and this act is just the opposite of relinquishment. We must be clear that in contemplation Christ controls the relationship. He comes when he chooses; he reveals himself as he sees best; he withdraws the intensity of his presence lest we seek to live on the emotion and ecstasy that his presence often generates.

And, when he hides himself from us, our urge to grasp him and contain him must be resisted. Just as we must resist the urge to reclaim previous experiences of consolation, letting go of all effort to retain present consolations is also essential. For me this has been particularly hard because of the way that I learned intimacy. My mother had been orphaned before she was five years old; a country doctor uncle reared her. But she never felt accepted in that family and never possessed anything that she felt was really hers. I heard her say many times that I was the first thing that she ever felt was truly her own.

My mother through her need for something that was truly hers clung to me. I responded by clinging to her. Her relationship to me fed something that she had longed for her whole life. As I recall my early years, I often felt drawn into a relationship of dependency and counter-dependence. This mutual dependence did not prove healthy for either of us. Her way of drawing me into herself provided my model for relating; I unconsciously drew others into myself.

Life in Christ demands letting go, not clinging. Christ does not make us dependent but inter-dependent.

Let go of the things to which you are clinging!

29
Living in God
"In him we live and move and have our being."
Acts 17:28

The world is inhabited by God and it is the environment needed for contemplation. The contemplative world has depth and meaning, life and color, proportion and beauty and it contains mystery too. This enchanted world of the Spirit contrasts sharply with the flat world of the rationalist – accidental, random, and meaningless. Contemplation sharpens our awareness of the God-filled world in which we live. Would a better metaphor be a God-alive world?

What a difference it would make in our contemplation if we could recover the reality that the world is immersed in the divine. Our longing for a home in the awareness of the divine reaches beyond the material and it does not turn the world into God. Pantheism is not our dream; God is not everything. Perhaps we long for panentheism – God in everything.

I wish that I could experience God in all things – in the life in a lily or the busy ant or the bird on the wing. Why cannot I see God in the majesty of a mountain or in the vastness of the ever expanding universe? What keeps me from seeing the Presence of the Holy in a stranger I meet or with a friend with whom I spend time? There are moments when I do see God in the world around me, but alas, those moments of awareness come too seldom.

Once I did see something of the divine in a beautiful plant. I gazed at its stem and leaf and imagined the life flowing in it. And, I wondered for a moment or two if the life in me was kin to the life in the plant. We both drew life from the same source and is it possible that the life in my soul related to the life in the plant? Both the leaf and I were created and sustained by the Energy of the One in whom we live and move and have our being.

This is the environment of contemplation, and contemplation is the way into a deepened awareness of the One in whom everything lives and moves and has its being.

Notice the life in the leaves, the trees, and the universe and realize your oneness.

30

Love in the Heart

"God's love has been poured into our hearts by the Holy Spirit."
Romans 5:5

The love of God in the heart lies at the center of our search. It came into us at birth and lay dormant until it was awakened by the Spirit of God. And the Catholic Church holds that Christ is implanted at baptism. In the best circumstances the love of God grows to maturity. In the evangelical tradition the love of God fills the heart of a believer and expands through personal knowledge of Christ and a deeper consecration. Whether in the evangelical or the liturgical tradition, contemplation opens the heart for the outpourings of God's love.

The most profound statement in the New Testament is found in the Apostle John's first letter: "Whoever does not love does not know God, for God is love." The teaching of the faith identifies love with God and the practice of love as the expression of God. Whether in the Catholic Tradition or the Evangelical Tradition, the Spirit is the agent of filling our hearts with love. This love, which is identified with God, flows freely into the heart of the contemplative in the solitude of silence.

In contemplation the mind becomes still, distractions disappear and a shift of consciousness occurs. The shift is like the turning of a page, like walking through a door into a different room, like stepping on a slanted, slippery floor and gently sliding deeper into the quiet. In these divine moments distractions do not disappear, but they are more easily controlled or even ignored. When we are brought into the divine presence, God fills this inner space of the soul with love. God pours love into us as an unearned gift and through us pours into the world embodied grace.

No wonder the mystics emphasize that the heart of contemplation is love.

In your waiting, be patient until the love comes and be persistent when you don't recognize it.

31

United to Him

"If we have been united with him in a death like his,
we will certainly be united with him in a resurrection like his."

Romans 6:5

Death and Resurrection are powerful metaphors pointing to the redemption and transformation of our lives. These metaphors cannot be exhausted as applied to those who have been reconciled. Engage them, draw on them, appropriate them in your soul again and again and they never diminish in their power.

These two profound symbols point to a ground that is deep enough and powerful enough to transform the whole world, the Church of Jesus Christ and every believer and follower of his. At its core transformation always means dying and rising. The old must die so that the new may arise. Old leaves fall from the tree so that new ones may grow in their place. Old social arrangements must pass so that new ones can come into acceptance. Present forms of the Church must dissolve for the new forms to come to birth. The present formation of our lives, like our ever changing bodies, must die so that new forms of being can be born.

The contemplative dies to his or her old ways of being in the world, as well as to the old ways of seeing it. When the soul penetrates the Creative Ground, new life erupts in the soul. God is the God of transformation and newness. We enter this creative depth through the road of 'unknowing,' which means death to all of our old ways of approaching God. Sometimes when the soul rests in this depth, newness breaks into the spirit. And often it is after the deep silence when our awareness tingles with a sense of the Holy. When we are least expecting any divine occurrence, the Spirit of new love and hope comes to us from God. Often it comes in the form of new energy or ideas or intuitions, like a resurrection of something that may have died.

Give yourself willingly to the process of death and resurrection!

32

Life in the Spirit

"But you are not in the flesh but in the Spirit, since the Spirit of God dwells in you."
Romans 8:9

The contemplative lives in the Spirit. To be in the Spirit means to be under the impulses of love and trust. It is life lived in attentiveness to God. This God-centered life springs from the presence of God that dwells in the deepest level of human consciousness. This life in God contrasts with life in the flesh, a life held in captivity to the selfish passions of human nature.

The Spirit in one sense has been part of our life from the moment of birth; it is part of being human, of having the capacity to sense the Beyond in the Here and Now. Though part of us, this Spirit may go unrecognized for years and in some persons the Spirit never gets attention. To become aware of the Spirit is an awakening of sorts that opens the human Spirit to the Divine, which brings a sense of Transcendence into the common place.

Human imagination often blocks the awakening by expecting the opening of the eyes of the soul to be such a powerful mystical experience that the memory is marked forever. Certainly, this may occur but it is also possible that the Spirit rises within us like warm water in the tub rises to cover us.

Living in this Spirit should never be marked with excessive effort. It is more letting go than it is grasping; it is more like floating than swimming.

In the deep silence we open our hearts to the indwelling Spirit and trust that this divine presence is transforming us. This indwelling Spirit of God functions in the deep stillness and focuses and unifies us. I believe this Spirit inspires gratitude for my life and for all the good things that have come to me. It is the Spirit that shows generosity to a frail young woman who waits tables in a local restaurant. This indwelling Spirit aches when I see persons I love choosing pathways that will lead them astray. When I appreciate the things of God more than the pleasures, achievements and relationships of earth, I believe the Spirit is at work in me.

Does this seem like living in the Spirit to you?

Notice what the Spirit is doing and keep yourself open to the Presence in you!

33
Guided

"For all who are led by the Spirit of God are the children of God."
Romans 8:14

The silence that makes us more deeply aware of the indwelling Spirit of God also directs our lives. The guidance of the Spirit does not violate our freedom because God does not take back so precious a gift. Neither does God want from us a compelled obedience. Divine guidance operates in the narrow space between human freedom and the divine will. The Spirit's guidance neither destroys freedom nor forces God's will upon us. The Spirit by intuition and persuasion shows us the next step on our journey.

I experience the leading of the Spirit as a subtle and very gentle movement like the breath of a child. Sometimes this guidance comes as an idea that at first seems my own, but it returns with a bit of urgency and seems to demand attention. An idea formed in my own mind and expressed in my own words turns out to be guidance. At other times thoughts come with such clarity and strength that immediately I recognize the Voice of God in them. The guidance of the Spirit functions also to help us recognize a temptation before it arrives full-blown. It appears like a cloud floating toward me, and in it I see a diversion from God and I am able to reject it before it arrives.

Sometimes the guidance comes through an encounter with other people. For example, you may be having coffee with a friend who has wished to speak about an issue in her church leadership role. After the discussion the question arises of what "our" church needs. In the course of describing perceived needs, the question of your role in that change arises. Suddenly, you begin to see your role differently. Inspiration comes to you with energy. You decide. When you look back upon the encounter, the conviction grows that the Spirit of God was present directing the conversation and enlightening your mind.

The Spirit's guidance seems to be a joint activity – the urges and disclosures of the Spirit and the discernment and a free response of personal choice.

From the desire of your heart seek earnestly to be led by God!

34

The Depth

"...for the Spirit searches everything, even the depths of God."
I Corinthians 2:10

The Spirit searches the depths of God and the depths of the human spirit. Like looking into a bag of treasures and pulling out the good and the beautiful, the Spirit searches the depths of God for only God knows God. The Spirit brings the presence of God into contact with the precise need of the patient seeker at the moment. In a single movement the Spirit reveals God so that the seeker comes to know God more deeply, but at one and the same time, the Spirit uncovers the depths of the human heart so that the person comes to know himself or herself in reality.

One day the Spirit showed me that I was a controlling soul. Though it did not seem to me that my ideas and directions felt controlling, in a moment I saw that if the same words were spoken to me, that is precisely how I would hear them -- controlling. When I brought this new awareness to Christ, he smiled. What compassion he must have, and what patience too. In a simple way this text points to the double search – the depths of God and the depths of the human soul!

Within all of us humans there is a degree of darkness. The pioneers of the Spirit affirm that for one to encounter God, he or she must make a journey through darkness. Because the Spirit knows the hidden depths of the heart and because the Spirit seeks to draw us to God, we must pass through the darkness where only faith will prevail. Be assured that though we cannot see God, nor can we feel the work of the Spirit, the searching goes on without our knowledge. To progress on this journey, it is necessary that we embrace the darkness and make our way through it. Beyond the darkness in the depth of human consciousness is the mirror of God through which we see God's reflection and ourselves.

Press against the darkness making your way into the depths and you will discover treasures old and new.

35

The Temple

"Do you not know that you are God's temple and that God's Spirit dwells in you?"
I Corinthians. 3:16

What image comes to your mind when you think of a temple? Is it the shape of the Jewish Temple, a Hindu Temple, or some particular church? Do you see the temple as a building?

The temple, no matter what faith, is more than a mere building. When you come near a temple, you know that you are on holy ground because the temple area is holy. The holiness of the temple, in part, derives from its being the place that worship is offered. Ah, but the holiness of the place and the worship of the place have a degree of holiness because the temple is the dwelling place of God. So more than the ground and more than the worship offered is the fact that God is present in the temple. The temple is the dwelling place of God.

In a letter to the Corinthian Church, St. Paul suggests that the true temple is the human heart by asking, "Do you not know that you are God's temple and that God's Spirit dwells in you?" God's temple is not the bricks and mortar of an edifice, but the warm tissues of the heart and the deep recesses of the mind. The God resident within us may be out of reach of the hand or the grasp of the mind, but dwelling in us nevertheless.

Not only does God dwell in each person, but God also dwells in the church, which is also a temple – the community is God's temple. So the embodiment of the Spirit is both corporate and personal – the Spirit dwells in the body of Christ and in the bodies that constitute it. Sacramentally, every baptized person participates in the Body of Christ; the union is created by God's Spirit. Experientially, the Body of Christ comes alive through meeting God in prayer and silence and in meeting each other member of the community in the Spirit.

Contemplation in community opens the doors for this transcendent meeting to occur for the gathered worshippers. When I attend a gathering, I look upon the community of my fellow-worshippers as an expression of Christ, Christ made visible and tangible. When I sit with them in prayer and praise, I think of one Voice worshipping the one God. And from time to time, it seems that this community is Christ on earth, here and now.

Be a temple in the Temple when you gather to worship.

131

36

In the Body

"Do you not know that your body is a temple of the Holy Spirit within you, which you have from God."

I Corinthians 6:19

Paul gives special emphasis to the locus of the Spirit – the human body. He urges that we glorify God in the body. For many years ascetic contemplation has treated the body as an obstacle to a deep fellowship with God; it has been seen as a deceitful enemy that draws believers away from God.

With this view becoming dominant, many serious seekers after God abused the body with fasting, sleeping on cold stones, lashing the body as punishment, and denying all bodily pleasures. This view of the body has roots in Plato and in Dionysus, the fifth century Syrian monk, who for many years was thought to be a companion of St. Paul. This radical rejection of the body as a hindrance to true spirituality denies the goodness of God's creation and should not be looked upon as the enemy of contemplation.

Let us be clear, God dwells in our bodies; they are not so fallen that God cannot inhabit them. Contemplation includes both an awareness of the body and a tender caring for the body. I want to be aware of the basic needs of the body – food, rest and proper exercise. And, I want to see God in the life and health of my body, both in how I care for and use the body I have received. And I want to glorify God in my body, which belongs to him. The presence of God in my body continues to transform it until one day it is like Christ's glorious body.

Loving and caring for the body is an aspect of loving Christ and serving God. We are our bodies.

Keep in loving awareness of your body and you will likely be aware of God in you!

37

Christ Lives in Me

"I am crucified with Christ, nevertheless I live,
yet not I but Christ lives in me."
Galatians 2:19-20

Consider these amazing paradoxes – crucified but alive, I live but not I, Christ lives in me, I live in him! Words failed the Apostle when he endeavored to describe the mutuality of the Christian life, so he resorts to paradox to force us to imagine what cannot be realized in any other way. His claims stagger reason, but he simultaneously liberates intuition and imagination so that we may receive just a hint of our unity with Christ.

The Apostle strongly desires for the Galatians and for us the appropriation of the shared life of Christ in our daily lives. At some point in our journey we begin to make efforts to express the compassion of Christ to those in pain, to bear the burdens of the weak and to welcome the stranger. When we begin to show these virtues, we experience a mutuality beyond human efforts – Christ in us, Christ for us and Christ through us.

The mature believer has become united with Christ so deeply that the life of sacrificial love becomes natural. And, perhaps best of all, the new "I" is aware that the old "I" no longer lives and the I that is in the image of God expresses Christ.

When we consider the aim of Christ to make us one with himself, it is not wearisome to wait for the manifestation of the Spirit in our silence. We can wait. We can listen. We can relinquish all claim to ourselves in order to wait before the God who comes in the silence to prepare us for this glorious union with Christ.

Pray to become so absorbed in him that he lives in you without your notice of it.

38

Self-Emptying

"Let the same mind be in you that was in Christ Jesus."
Philippians 2:5

What a treasure it would be to have the mind of Christ! Having his mind we would be free of grasping after power or recognition. We would be neither self-exalting nor self-deprecating. The mind of Christ is filled with peace and confidence. He possessed a confidence that despite what happened to him, the compassionate love of God came to him enabling him to triumph. Grant us this mind.

We have no way to attain this mind; we cannot climb up to heaven and bring it down from above. We cannot practice a discipline that will create it in us. Even faithfulness through the passing years will not attain the mind that was in Christ Jesus. Yet, we can pray, "God grant me this mind."

In all our years we have found him faithful and true. Never does he create a desire to tantalize or deceive us. Never has he revealed a grace and chosen to withhold it. Never has he suggested a possibility and permitted me to fall short of it. Let us rest in this confidence until the mind of Christ is formed in us.

God grants to the family the mind of Christ in numerous ways – for some a grace, for others a miracle, and still for others an imperceptible transformation. The mind of Christ will be formed in us most fully through contemplation. God grant us this mind.

"Let this mind be in you." Letting means permitting, an open-the-door act to let it come in. "Letting" rules out all methods, all techniques, and all rituals. Letting is letting, like pulling the plug lets the water drain from the tub or like placing a bucket under a tap and letting the water fill it. Letting is something less than a self-conscious choice; it is simply recognizing that the "letting" has already occurred and the mind of Christ is indeed in us. Thanks be to God for those times that Christ thinks in our thoughts, discerns through our perceptions, and chooses the lowly place for us. This is indeed the Mind of Christ.

"Let the mind of Christ dwell in me."

Pay attention to your thoughts and wonder if some of them are his! And, attend your feelings also!

134

Pushing the Edges

1. Always Beginning!

For all of us there is a first step, beginning if you will, in our walk toward contemplation. Many of us make a diligent effort to move forward in our prayer, but for others of us, contemplation comes as a spontaneous experience and persists with very little effort. Wherever we find ourselves on this journey, we had a starting point, a beginning. Most persons who are on the way experience a strangeness in their early days on the path. Each day it is the same; we are beginning again. Merton has a strong word for us all. He says that "we will never be anything else but beginners, all our life." So if we feel rather odd in our efforts, if it seems that we are getting nowhere and making no progress on our journey, maybe it is because we are beginners and always will be.

The word, beginner, floods my mind with numerous images – the first time to ride a bike, the first day at school, the first solo drive in a car -- to name a few. The things that I recall as "beginner experiences" in the spiritual life include: saying "yes" to Christ, offering a prayer in the hearing of others, and speaking of my faith to a friend. Most of us have memories of these firsts. These first acts form a pattern to which we have added new insights and practices.

We are painfully aware of our inexperience and ineptness as a beginner in the practice of faith; yet we realize it is the only way it could be. But in contemplation it bothers us that we can never advance beyond being a beginner. Each day we are beginning again, nothing stored up from the day before, everything is fresh and new.

To be a beginner in riding a bike or giving a Christian witness does not attack our self-esteem because we can develop a degree of excellence in riding or sharing our faith. Not so with contemplation. Contemplation does not lend itself to techniques, formal plans, or well-marked paths.

Excellence must not even be a goal for us, so faithfully we begin again each day. There is no way to take charge of our contemplation.

If we could master contemplation, it would not be contemplation of the God revealed in Jesus, nor the God of infinite mystery. Any so-called competence in contemplation would be a god of our own creation and a prayer directed by our own efforts. The very idea of maturity or perfection violates the practice of contemplative prayer. True contemplation follows the path of submission and surrender, the way of unknowing and of trust. If we ever become contemplatives, it will be by "beginning again," each day a different step, each day a surprise and each day an adventure along an unmarked path.

Let us then content ourselves with being beginners in the art of contemplation, for that is truly what we are and what we will be for the rest of our lives. I find an innocent joy in being a beginner. I'm not expected to be perfect. I do not know the way because there is no way. What freedom comes with beginning the practice of silence and stillness with no goals, no agenda, and no expectations! Because I am a beginner I do not know where the first step will lead me. As a beginner, I am curious about what lies ahead; but it remains hidden. I anticipate the marvelous adventure before me, but I neither design it or control my steps. I enter a world of wonder and enchantment where everything is upside down.

As I start in earnest my contemplation of God, I accept my status as a beginner – I do not know where I am going or how to get there. I am free to begin again and again. I am on a road that leads to its own destination. I am a beginner, always beginning again!

Will you join me on this journey? I invite you also to become a beginner on this journey to nowhere.

2. Hearing without Listening

Most of all the contemplative "listens in silence." In my efforts to walk the contemplative path I find that I listen at different levels. I usually begin by listening to my body – aware of tensions, pain and tightness. Awareness often dissolves the stress. Then, I listen to the buzz in my mind – the stirring of ideas and clamoring of distracting thoughts. I try hard to get still deep down inside and surrender myself. I know that trying too hard does not help me on the way to stillness. As I cease my efforts, I am often taken to a deeper silence — mind alert, heart open and spirit receptive to GodSpeech. Most often this attentive listening is rewarded with a greater silence. Silence itself becomes a language.

The silence is wordless speech that enlarges my spirit and deepens my conviction of being clothed in the mystery that I cannot define or direct. Most of the time I hear nothing from God in this deep silence. I have no complaint; I have listened with 'unhearing' ears -- no sounds, words or discernable intuitions.

Yet, when I emerge from the deep silence, something comes with me. Merton suggests that "we most truly begin to hear God when we have ceased to listen." Often I return to the landscape of daily life with a stronger sense of peace; I have a conviction that I belong in this world and that I am part of a purpose larger than myself. Are these transformations indicative of God's work of recreation?

Also, after an encounter with the deep silence, when I am least expecting it, a clear communication forms in my mind. This revelation in my heart assures me that I am not alone or inspires me to take the next step or provides a directive for my life. Yesterday these words flowed gently into my mind after an engagement with the silence: "Trust in my unfailing presence!" Sometimes I hear when I'm not particularly listening. It seems that small changes are occurring in me as I daily "begin again" to follow this ancient way of being before God: a deeper awareness of God's presence, a gentle silencing of unbecoming speech, and a kinder, more generous spirit..

3. No Logic in Prayer

Contemplation does not follow the laws of logic; it is not a practice or a position or a relationship that we can blueprint and reproduce. The deeper experiences of prayer occur in the sphere of unknowing and in the arena of impotency. The merciful God does what we cannot do and the changes gently emerge in our consciousness. Who can explain how God touches the human spirit and transforms our desires and reactions?

For a good many years, I had no power to cope with death. Since my childhood, the awareness of finitude, combined with a shattering sense of eternity, plagued me with a joy-shattering torment. When I was about sixty-five years of age, I awakened to a freedom from this angst. This transformation came as a gift without my consciously asking for it or recognizing exactly when it arrived. Suddenly, I realized I no longer feared death or the boundlessness of eternity, and I had a growing anticipation of the next phase of being.

With this freedom came a deep consciousness of peace. Inside the boundaries of that peace, I confronted a puzzle. For some reason living forever did not matter, it was no longer a goal! This freedom sharply contrasted with my early motivation for being a Christian – to go to heaven, to have eternal life and to be delivered from hell. If God has a place for me in the Eternal Scheme of Things, I will be grateful, but the anxiety of not being has left me, and I experience a freedom previously unknown. I found or was given (I'm not sure which) a peace with not being.

As I have continued on this path, it has begun to appear to me that the lines that separate good and bad, true and false, right and wrong have blurred. I seem to intuit life as a whole rather than splitting it into pieces. Distinctions that I once made clearly and decisively changed into varying degrees of good or evil or opposites held together by a dialectical tension. My spirit tends more toward inclusion than toward exclusion, toward one rather than the many.

The lines between Christ and other faiths seem to be fading. I have no inclination to discount Jesus Christ. I am a Christian and will die a believer in him as the Son of God, but I do not condemn all other religions. God is present and at work among all people and people groups. I believe Christ is present incognito inviting all persons into wholeness and fulfillment whether or not they know his name.

Observing these once clear demarcations beginning to crumble brings with it a feeling of risk and subtle disease; this experience nearly always accompanies profound transformations. The life energy flowing through all of us and within all of us creates changes, and changes bring new ways of seeing our world and participating in it. Without growth and change, life petrifies. I can only believe Christ leads me down this pathway into this transition.

4. Scriptural Foundation

In my wondering about the validity of waiting in silence before God, this statement came to me: "For the Spirit searches everything, even the depths of God." (I Cor. 2:10) It is not my spirit that searches out the depths of God, but God's Spirit seeks out the depths in me. The Spirit searches both human depths and Divine depths.

Paul wrote about the wisdom of God, which earthly rulers do not perceive, and we recognize this wisdom because the searching Spirit gives it to us. Paul speaks of wisdom as he speaks of mystery, the unfathomable mystery of God. Mystery blends with wisdom in Paul's understanding of the Spirit's revelation of this incomprehensible God.

On one occasion the divine appears in the mighty acts of creation and the beauty of nature. Doubtless the Spirit selects multiple ways to unveil the divine mystery, and one of those would be through the contemplation of God. When we enter into the realm of the sacred, it is the Spirit that invites us. As our host, the Spirit shows us what we have not seen, nor thought, nor felt or even imagined. The One who knows my depths as well as the depths of God brings us into a relationship with this unimaginable God that is beyond understanding. Through the agency of the Spirit we are ushered into a communion with God that we do not achieve because it is unachievable, yet it is given freely.

This communion with God occurs in the silent depth beyond the reach of awareness. The human spirit may even feel asleep while the Spirit operates with absolute precision. Generally, we cannot name the Spirit's action nor can we see immediate changes. We do have a growing confidence that the Spirit is transforming our consciousness, which is manifest in our choices and responses.

The weakness of our humanity keeps seeking for evidence that we are actually meeting God. We are driven to look for signs of the divine presence in the feeling of peace and tranquility. We hope that little impulses to change indicate the work of the Spirit. These signs may actually provide exactly what we long for, but the time comes when we are stripped of signs and thrust into the land of "unknowing," and it is here we learn the way of love that leans on naked faith. Naked faith means that we believe God in the absence of signs, wonders, miracles, and consolations. The searching Spirit seems to be thoroughly familiar with this landscape.

5. Christ the Way

Anyone can meditate on signs, light or beauty, but Christians enter into the Sacred Realm through the agency of Jesus Christ. Though it is a stumbling block to many, Jesus did say: "I am the way, the truth and the life." Without pronouncing judgment upon those who walk other pathways, Jesus Christ stands before the Christian as the way into God's presence – Way, Truth, Life, Door, Light, Resurrection. Even when making this claim, I do not imply that Christ is not standing before those who walk a different path or that he is not present to those who use different words and symbols to speak of their journeys.

Christians experience him as WAY when in Bethany he raises Lazarus. To those standing by he says, "I am the resurrection..." Through his spiritual presence he raises us who are unconscious of God into a living awareness of the divine in our midst and in our hearts. So our imagination shifts from thinking of him as resurrection to experiencing him as resurrection -- being raised into the presence of God. When we enter into the Father's presence, the son accompanies us. He escorts us into the presence of God.

Under the metaphor of Light, Christ illuminates our pathway, directs us into contemplation: "I am the light of the world; those who follow me shall not walk in darkness but shall have the light of life." (John 8:12) Or, in another place John says, "God is light..." (I John 1:5) In our meditation we follow Christ into the light of God, whose very being is Light. And, the psalmist presses the metaphor when he utters the prayer, "With you is the fountain of life; in your light we see light." (Ps. 36:9) In contemplation we abide in the luminous presence as it bathes and cleanses our whole being.

In contemplation Christians see God through the lenses of Christ, and this seeing becomes "unseeing" in the presence of God's blazing light. Because he is our guide we do not get lost in the darkness or fall into the abyss. In him we are secure as we seek the depths of the mystery through the guidance of Jesus Christ who is our principle of discernment in the midst of our shifting experience.

6. The Guide

Contemplation is not discovering a way to God; it is being taken by the hand and guided to a place that lies outside our sphere of knowledge. For the beginner no insight holds greater significance than the recognition that we do not know the way into God's immediate presence. God takes us by the hand and leads us in the darkness by a way that we do not know and, therefore, could never hope to travel apart from this experienced guide. Without the assistance of this guide we would find ourselves hopelessly in the darkness. We cannot 'learn' the way of contemplation through our accumulated experience or even a discerning memory. God wills each entry into the Sacred to be a unique experience and we cannot make our own rules, lay out the proper disciplines or find a human director to show us the way. God alone leads to God!

The God of Mystery does guide us. When we are least expecting it, a hand reaches out of the darkness to gently guide us; the breath of holy desire breathes upon us; and, though we cannot see the path, we believe that our feet are traveling on the right road as the Way keeps opening before us and through the beckoning of our Guide we make the right turns.

This hand that guides us to the place of sublime intimacy with God unites our "soul image" and our "God-hunger." If we knew the way, we would likely run past our Guide or dismiss him. We would seek our heart's desire without regard for our dependence on the Guide and would end up following our way instead of God's way. Even though we may have walked a long way in the same direction, we have accumulated no wisdom that will take us to the place to which we long to go.

Every day marks a new beginning and even the knowledge of yesterday, like the manna in the desert, has begun to grow mold. We have no good choice but to follow our guide and to eat the bread of endurance, which is received on each day's leg of the journey. Surely our Guide will steady us when we stumble and pick us up when we fall.

When we are guided by God, we have no way of knowing if we are arriving at our destination because we do not know the destination, nor do we know the landscape along the way. Because we are traversing new territory, we implicitly trust the hand of the Guide.

7. A Contemplative Orientation

There is a difference between being a contemplative and having a contemplative outlook. Merton says that not everyone can be a contemplative but everyone can have a contemplative outlook. Some people, like monks, who have been called to the life of prayer spend much of their day in the silence. Daily they are drawn deeper and deeper into the mystic way until they find a unity with God that enables them to live constantly in a profound awareness of the divine. Being a contemplative is not a vocation that we can take upon ourselves. According to Merton the real contemplatives will always be rare.

Though pure contemplatives may be few, many, if not all, can have a contemplative outlook and learn to be receptive to contemplative experience. All of us can enter into a new way of "seeing" that changes our perspective. This way of "seeing" the world and one's life in it originates at the same source -- the Divine Presence. We make the journey into silence and find ourselves in 'the cloud of unknowing,' but we inevitably return to the world of sound and things and people with an altered consciousness. The personal awareness, previously dominated by images, rituals and logic, no longer possesses the old certitude. This potent way of 'unknowing' subverts the old way of knowing and opens the soul to new dimensions of the divine mystery – the pervasive infinite manifestation of the invisible God in each moment, plus the manifestation of the unmanifest mystery of God.

Two strong influences shape the contemplative outlook: the mystery of God manifest in the present moment and the unmanifest God, which is hidden in the same moment. The contemplative outlook embraces the present moment as God's gift and seeks to realize the presence of God in everything; this outlook also wonders at the divine mystery. The contemplative outlook on occasion delves beneath the surface to engage the unmanifest mystery, only to return with greater sensitivity to the manifest mystery seen and heard and felt in the moment.

By contrast the true contemplative relentlessly casts off all attachments as he or she travels the way of unknowing into the silence where words are seldom heard and images fade into the unmanifest mystery, into the Void of the Holy. The contemplative possesses the vision, follows the intuitions of the Spirit and engages the Self beyond the self in ways that resist conceptualization but are, nevertheless, real.

8. Prayer of the Heart

Contemplation is praying from the heart; it is giving expression to the deepest within us to that which is ultimately beyond us. The prayer of the heart consists in that ever-present yearning for God – to be present to God, to realize God, to be known by God.

In my earlier days I took seriously Paul's admonition to pray without ceasing. My efforts consisted of thinking about God at least every quarter hour or recalling God when I felt the tiny, aluminum cross that I carried in my pocket. Then I learned the Jesus Prayer and I repeated it: "Lord Jesus Christ, Son of God, have mercy on me a sinner." This type of disciplined prayer was a way of seeking to be with God through the medium of words and images. I invested quite a bit of effort in praying without ceasing.

I could never say that these simple disciplines held no value for my spiritual growth and my learning to pray. They were my best efforts to be faithful to God, to place God always before my face, but my prayer was with too much effort. I sought to be near to God and my vigorous attempts resembled panting more than slow, measured, natural breathing.

Finley's depiction of the manifestation of God in the present moment opens me to an awareness of the Presence in a simpler, less effortful way. To come to the present moment, to be present to this moment with a sharpened awareness, enables me to realize that God is happening to me now.

In this present moment I turn toward the desire of my heart, I listen for the prayer that Christ is forming within me or I simply become inwardly still, recollected. The consciousness of God and my desire for God become my prayer. In this prayer of the heart I find a wonderful, gentle freedom like a bird flying from an open hand or a stream of water cascading down a hillside. I am not seeking to pray beyond myself nor above myself but from within myself. (Psalm 131) I am letting the prayer that I already am happen. In this prayer I am neither seeking to get favors or gifts; nor do I seek to change my circumstances. I am praying myself, praying my true identity by acknowledging the Spirit's prayer within me. When I pray in this fashion my spiritual life is not separated from my natural life; they are one.

Is this not the prayer of the heart expressing our identity with God? Is not it "the deepest ground of our identity with God"?

9. A Gift of the Prayer

The prayer of the heart lies on the border of contemplation; it draws on the simplicity and sincerity of the heart's deepest longing. This prayer is nothing more than spontaneous desire directed toward God.

But in a richer, fuller sense, the prayer of the heart, which we notice as a God-inspired yearning, eventually draws us beyond feelings, words and human understanding; it is a special gift. Like all gifts this one, too, "should never be taken for granted."

My earliest efforts at prayer focused on holding an image of God in my mind. I felt the need for a picture of the One I addressed in prayer. The images arose like seed from the soil and rotated in my mind cultivated by a gentle hand – Father, King, Lord, Mother. The character of Christ, as concretely manifest in his life and teaching, personified "God with us." Christ was transparent to the divine presence and permitted it to shine through him without distortion. Eventually, I discovered that the images, which had become the furniture filling my conceptual living room, did not evoke the prayer of the heart. To pray with the heart does not even require images; it is face-to-face without an image or a representation of any kind. Prayer dissolves into a profound communion with the Invisible.

The prayer that flows spontaneously from the heart surpasses all images. Though images may serve us well for a large part of the journey, there comes a time to relinquish our favorite concepts and pictures. These mental emblems should not be discounted to others or withheld from them, but like crutches, there will come a time to discard them.

The prayer of the heart arises through spontaneous acts of Grace. Gifts cannot be demanded or they cease to be gifts. Gifts are chosen by the Giver and are distributed at the Giver's discretion. The prayer of the heart is such a gift from God; the prayer of the heart is to be received as a gift from the Giver without taking either for granted. Eventually the prayer of the heart does not feel like prayer at all because the Other has become part of us; God has given Godself to us.

10. Simplicity and Sincerity

Though the pathway of contemplation may be obscure to the casual observer and indescribable to all but poets, simplicity and sincerity mark its boundaries. The contemplative attitude begins with sincerity; it has been stripped of all sham and pretense because it has seen how masks, calculated acts, and shortcuts only deceive the pretender, no one else, and surely not God. The dark night of faith also has stripped the heart of illusions so that it no longer seeks or wishes false fulfillment. Without a charade the heart expresses its deep longing for God like a child pleading with her mother. If the response to our longing tarries, the contemplative, like a mature adult seasoned by suffering, does not worry or become discontented. Rather, the longing heart patiently awaits an answer and if none is forthcoming, it contentedly waits. Having asked before and sought its own answer, it has learned in the dark to trust the answer given, even if it is sheer silence. Knowing its desires and God's loving care, the sincere heart does not fear delay, which may, in fact, be God's answer.

Most of us who have any sincerity at all have wondered about the meaning of simplicity. What is it? Perhaps it is a combination of simple words like "I love you" or "Your will be done." Even simpler, perhaps it is a profound inner ache for God, a pain deeper than words, arising from the place where words originate. But could simplicity also be like a cat stretched out in the sunshine, simply sitting or lying in the light of the divine presence? Is not sitting or lying or waiting less complex than longing or speaking? Make me like the relaxed, contented cat that soaks up the sun, the one that "is" in the light without much bother about it. The psalmist surely knew this experience when he wrote, "like a weaned child with its mother; my soul is like the weaned child that is with me." (Ps. 131:2)

Sincerity and simplicity are not virtues that we possess; they are what we are. We cannot possess sincerity; if we possessed it, quite quickly it would become an instrument for manipulation. Rather, we are sincere; it is woven into the fabric of our being; it is not a detachable trait used at will. These twin virtues become a part of us; they can never become strategies or techniques. Being sincere and simple is just the way we are and it is just the way that contemplation is done.

11. Unconditional Surrender

At some point on the pathway to contemplation, each voyager confronts a narrow gate with a low overhang; he or she must bend low and turn sidewise to squeeze through or turn back. Bending low and turning sidewise point to unconditional and total surrender to God; it implies an acceptance of our life and everything in it. These images reveal a deep truth, yet in our struggle to hear this truth, it is with great difficulty that we learn to open ourselves to it. In other situations

147

people might ask, "Does embracing one's situation as the will of God mean that our circumstances are always God's will?" For example, does this mean that God has placed the poor in their helplessness? Does it mean that God creates deformed babies? Does God will persons who are alienated from power to accept their plight without question?

This demand cut most deeply into me at the time of my divorce. Did God intend me to stay in an unworkable marriage? When I was struggling over the decision to ask her to marry me, I turned to the scripture for guidance. One morning I read, "You shall not take a wife in this place." These words went unheeded. Did I disobey God in taking a wife? Or, would I have honored God more fully by having spent my life in a hell of conflict? If the answer is "Yes," I have come too far to go back. That bridge has been crossed. Can I even now embrace my life as given and willed by God? Or, can I believe that God rescued me from the pain of a bad marriage and set me in a new place?

For today to become the day of New Beginning, I must begin with who I am and where I am in the unfolding of my life. This means that today I accept the role in my church as given by you. It also means that I accept all my relationships with generous and committed friends as your gifts. My wife also is your gift along with our children, resources, and opportunities. If I am to enter a life of contemplation I must realize that my state of soul, with its "unknowing" and my life with its joy and pain, is willed by you in this moment.

I am where I belong. My life is what it is. I can only pray, "God, I humbly surrender to you in the varied aspects of my life." It is this person and this life you have willed, even though my doubts war against the simple trust. Yet, as I live in this present moment of joy I have no knowledge of what the next moment will bring. I believe that it can bring nothing that is not willed for me.

12. Who Am I?

I am a word spoken by God, but I am not the first word. Of the first word there is no recorded history; it was even spoken before the utterance of "Let there be..." The first word, this primal word spoken before the beginning of the ages, was the WORD of God. "In the beginning was the Word and the Word was face to face with God and the Word was God." (John 1: 1-1)

I am not a primal word because the logos was from the beginning. He was of the very essence of God and indeed was the first Word. All things came into being through him and apart from him nothing had being at all. In him was life and the life in him sparked light in all persons he made.

God spoke this primal Word and it has echoed from eternity to the present and this Word reverberates in me and expresses itself through me. I am not the primal WORD but only an echo.

Words name things, they express actions, and they also describe and define. I am noun-like in that I am a thought of the Creator. Following hard upon this claim, it must be said that every other person is likewise a tangible word. If I want to know God, to contemplate God, I must listen to the unique revelation in these words both in myself and in others.

Verbs are words, too. Verbs express action. The action words of God do not remain statically locked in cages, they move. These acting words fill the universe with motion, energy and change. The verbs of God's vocabulary include hands-on production, the imaginative construal of meanings and expressions of creativity. I am a verb of God when I become part of God's action in the world. (All of us are actions; we simply do not recognize it.)

In this world of incarnate words every utterance modifies all other living words. Is this a reason why we are admonished to love one another? So bonded together all these sounds express the cacophony of God resounding throughout the universe.

And, what does this mean for our contemplation? Could it possibly mean that eventually we will live in awareness of being expressions of God?

13. Hidden in Nothingness

All contemplation aims for the glory of God. The glory of God flows from the true Self into the whole person affecting our whole demeanor. Embracing this Self demands more than knowing about it or viewing reflections of it in the eyes of others or sorting out its misdirected dreams and wishes. These illusions will deter us from the recovery of our true Self and the pure worship of God and becoming embodiments of the Divine Spirit.

The search for this elusive identity faces the persistent challenge of forging a way through the darkness to find the Self that lies in obscurity in the depth of the soul! Our search is hampered by both our ignorance of this Self and our fear of discovering it. Our various false selves in their substitute roles effectively conceal who we truly are. The popular culture also obscures the knowledge of this Self; it continuously broadcasts false images of the Self as the seeker for safety, security, recognition or godlike autonomy. These distorted images confuse the true seeker and divert the quest for authenticity to a surface fulfillment.

In addition to the lure of false images, the constant fear of what lurks in the shadows sorely tempts us to turn back. How can we make the journey through the darkness where we cannot see our way? How do we battle our ignorance and fear that keep us in confusion? Do we not often fear that snakes and lizards and creeping things hide in the darkness of our submerged self? If we encounter them or if they break our long established resistance, we only find the courage to go on when led by Another. God will surely lead us through the darkness surrounding the true Self!

To get us through this darkness, the Light of him who is the Light of the World will take us by the hand and lead us through the darkness; he will expose the illusions that distract us; and he will slay the dragons of fear and doubt that paralyze our movement. Repeatedly, if we turn to him in openness, he will come into us and make his home in us. Never grasping him or even imaging him, but allowing him to guide us to the Center wherein lies our true Self. Merton tells us that our true self is hidden in obscurity and 'nothingness' at the center where we are in direct dependence on God.

The light of the world enlightens every person who comes into the world. And, in this Light we see light.

14. Called Into Freedom
God calls us to freedom, a liberation for which all of us humans seek as surely as water seeks its level. Why must I be called to this liberation? Am I not seeking it? Do I not long for it? What is the call? Only the call of God truly liberates; it is freedom that appears in response to God's move toward me. God calls us into freedom because we find so many ways to become enslaved – blinded by our own egos, bound by alien

desires, which make us insensitive to our true identity. In this frozen
estate the Spirit calls us to our true home, a place where we can freely be
ourselves, the Selves we were created to be. Our identity and liberation
lie hidden in this beckoning of God, this drawing to Godself that does
not occur only once or all at once. We have been called in Christ and
this call to be a disciple had a beginning, but it will have no ending. The
call comes constantly, without interruption so that our identity never
fully crystallizes or gets completed. Like the call itself each of us is
constantly emerging from the shadow land of self-absorption into the
light of our destiny through the freedom we receive in our response to
God's call.

God's call is like a key that opens our cells, unshackles us and invites
us to move freely. God calls us to be who we already are, and to be that
person gives us the greatest freedom we can imagine. How simple, how
natural to choose our deepest desires for authenticity! In this freedom
there is no need to be especially religious, to seek out a particular piety
or to even have an image of the Self we are. We do not seek to be
religious but to be responsive to God.

God's call is like the wind caught by the sails, it provides power to
move the ship toward its destination. God's call is like the quacking of a
duck hen that anxiously seeks to call together her ducklings. It beckons
in the direction we are to go.

When I was younger I heard this call in the text of scripture, through
the urging of the Spirit, and also from the mouths of mentors and role
models. Now that I am old I hear the call in the silence – the "wordless"
call. In the deep silence I hear the call to live into my freedom as a child
of God! I respond to this call by setting out on the way of "unknowing."
I advance as I choose to be the Self that I am. Marching on "Freedom's
Road" I gladly become what I was destined to be. On this way I am in
this present moment, I am who I am destined to become.

15. Freedom To Love

Freedom in the Spirit means liberation to love. This love-seasoned
freedom runs counter to the popular notion that freedom unshackles us
from all restraints to follow random impulses. Such a profligate use of
freedom leads into greater bondage of all kinds. But freedom expressed in
love opens more deeply the channels of spontaneity and expressive living.

Merton describes this freedom as embracing "God's will in its naked, often impenetrable mystery." The words "naked and impenetrable" have a magnetic attraction for me. The "naked" will of God suggests a divine intention that has not yet been clothed in flesh, an intention looking for embodiment. It is an invisible power. Embracing God's will in its nakedness evokes the kind of trustfulness that knows not where the path of obedience will lead or how it will appear in a living, acting person. This naked embrace leads the trusting soul into an exhilarating expectancy of what lies ahead; it is a super-charged hope.

When the naked intent for God arrives at the doorway of consciousness as an irresistible thought, it often makes no sense; it seems disconnected from our present circumstance. When it appears as a yearning for love or a yearning for union, this, too, is hidden as deeply in mystery as the irresistible thought. The awareness of God's intent for us to abandon ourselves and allow the center of our world to shift from self to God always takes us to the edge of the unknown. Stepping across the line into darkness demands greater and greater abandonment of self and a deeper and deeper trust. Even when the intent of God comes as a direct command, the direction may be clear, but the outcome remains unknown. Mystery!

The naked intent of God arrives at our doorway wrapped in an impenetrable mystery; it is the mystery of God's own person and purpose. We can never penetrate the mystery of the divine mind even when it discloses itself. No matter how this mystery arrives, whether as yearning for the unnamed or a persistent thought or an opportunity to give unselfishly or a direct command to choose or act, it arrives as a mystery. It arrives as mystery because we do not know from whence it comes and whither it leads. Even a faithful response to the call leaves us with unanswered questions. We perceive this gracious call in the concreteness of the present moment and blindly take only one step at a time into the darkness that hides the path.

Contemplation opens our awareness and permits this impenetrable disclosure to come and to grasp us with conviction strong enough to spark our action in a wild freedom. In freedom we embrace the call, clothe it with a loving response, and express it as love for our brothers or sisters in obedience to God. The freedom that the Spirit creates retains its unrestrained nature when expressed in love. Can we not see how this freedom liberates us to experience directly the mystery of our lives?

Contemplation provides the environment for freedom to be manifest and love to be exercised and meaning to be created.

16. Ground of the Self

Contemplation leads us into the ground of the self, the true Self. Contemplation in all its forms contains ambiguous fundamentals. It seeks a contemplative depth that leads to union with God, but it remains unwilling for that depth to be vague, formless feelings. This persistent reflection enters into the divine mystery of our being to seek an understanding of God's gracious will and mercy as well as our utter dependence upon God. Merton says, "I penetrate the inmost ground of my life, seek the full understanding of God's will for me, of God's mercy to me, of my absolute dependence on him."

I, too, desire this pathway into the innermost ground of my life and I want to walk this path no matter where it leads or what it requires. Yet, to press forward, to surrender all rationalizing and to learn unflinching openness to God's will requires a gigantic step: I must be willing to be led by God.

Even when we choose this God-directed life, do we dare believe that God's will is being done in us now in the concreteness of this present moment? Instead of praying for a mysterious revelation of the divine will, we learn to pray that our eyes will be opened to see the manifestation of God's intention that presents itself in the circumstances, occurrences and challenges of our daily existence. Perhaps the time has now come to cease our seeking for what we already possess and recognize that the intent of God is already embodied in the concreteness of our ordinary lives.

As we journey into the ground of our lives and the scales fall from our eyes, we must courageously look in the face of God's long given mercy. Mercy has been shown us in ways we have not yet realized. How many times has our life been spared and we knew nothing of it? How deeply have we been forgiven without sufficiently expressed gratitude? From whence came courage to make risky decisions and live through them? Do not all of us long to penetrate the inmost ground of our lives deeply enough to get hints of this hidden mercy?

153

Intellectually, we know that everything depends upon the Divine intention and gracious mercy -- our life, our relations and our dreams and hopes. What would it mean to penetrate this inmost ground and discover where our contingent being connects with the "infinity of the mystery"?

Enduring answers to the questions that meditation brings up cannot be discovered stated and preserved like algebraic equations. The answers that we seek are "lived" realizations that appear as we persist on our journey to the center.

17. Always Present In Us

The designation of God as the Ground of Being tends to blur the personal aspects of the Divine, but it does offer a holistic vision of God and Creation in which created human beings retain a relationship with the Creator. God as the Ground of Being points to the fact that all Creation has its origin, subsistence and purpose in God. Ground is that out of which everything comes into being and grows. And further, God as the Ground of our being implies that life and meaning and creativity all come from God, everything comes from the source.

To further elaborate this vision, picture the unconscious mind as the depth of the soul that opens out into the Ground of being, the infinity of the mystery of God. As our Ground, God is continuously present to the unconscious dimension of the psyche, and through it indirectly influences consciousness with thoughts, images, and longings. This presence, though always present and active, is, nevertheless, invisible to the eyes of the soul. Into this invisible ground contemplation takes us, not by imagining or reasoning or willing, but by being completely open to this mysterious ground.

The contemplative seeks to descend through the layers of differentiated consciousness and to rest on the base line of this personal depth. Most of the daily journey may be spent in quieting the turbulent waves of consciousness so that the soul may wait confidently and expectantly for the Spirit to do the work of God within it. On this borderline of primal consciousness God draws the soul into momentary union with Godself – God in the Soul and the soul in God. Though we do not fully understand God's intention, and certainly we do not control God's actions, genuine transformation takes place in the depth, in the silence. The transformation is a cleansing and purifying act of God that simultaneously affects our relationship with God and with people.

The Ground of our being is also the Ground of every person's being and the ground of all things. As our ground God appears in the urges that move us in certain directions like caring for a street person or visiting a neighbor. When we follow these urges, we experience the actions of providence that caused us to meet people and respond to them. The One who grounds our being also directs the flow of energy and we become aware of marvelous things occurring.

Scant evidence of transformation begins to appear: the budding of Christian virtues, an increase of inner strength, consciousness of ethical behavior and the love of a community of fellow journeyers. A deeper concern for the world begins to shape our existence: respect for human dignity, energy for creativity, the search for peace and justice, and a deep sense of belonging in the universe. The realization of these manifestations of the Spirit gives just a bit of confidence that we are moving along the right pathway. We begin to have more hope that our contemplation will indeed bring us into the realm of the Sacred and shape within us a sense of ultimate belonging.

18. Deepened Consciousness

Contemplation is the deliberate act of thinking about God, and its source may be sacred writings, our lives or nature. With an awareness sharpened by reading or reflecting, we more often notice our connectedness to God. In each instance we must take care not to make the media ends but always retain their status as means – means that foster our awareness of God.

The lines between meditation and contemplation often become blurred. Thoughts on the beauty or symmetry of nature meld with the beautiful, and our once specific hard-edged thoughts merge with the Ground of the Beautiful, and the distinct lines disappear in the encounter with God.

The expanded awareness comes as a gift, not as a reward. The discipline of attentiveness clears the clutter of our hearts so that God may act. The intensified love and the sharpened faith are gifts of God. Our preparation simply enables us to recognize them. The closer we draw to God, the more fully we are convinced that acts of love and lives of faithfulness derive from God's gracious gift of presence.

Sometimes our consciousness is sharpened to the point that the presence is almost palpable but even when it is not so obvious, it remains as a second thought, the one always standing in the background of other interests.

There will never be a time when we cease to place ourselves at the Center to hear God. God does delight in the souls that wait and wait!

19. Humility Before God

Humility abides in the heart of Christ. He who was in the image of God emptied himself, assumed the form of a servant and became a human. As a man he never claimed the power available to him, and even permitted his enemies to kill him. Self-emptying produces beauty of character but to many of us, it seems so distant. Yet, daily we have numerous occasions when we could embrace the lowly way.

Daily the opportunity for humility presents itself to us – an unreasonable demand from a friend or a receptionist asks to put us on hold, a request for money from a street person, and the annoying reactions from a friend, a spouse or a boring acquaintance. Each of these invitations to humility could grind away some of our self-assertiveness, the false attitude that we have a right to be respected and honored. We say that we wish to be humble, but in turn reject the opportunities daily presented to us.

The humility that does not demand its own way, that does not feel superior to the receptionist, stranger or street person, that wills God's will time and again; this humility provides the heartbeat of prayer and life with God. When God sees this humility there must be a rush to join his child at the bottom of the ladder, the child who with undemanding trust looks up and waits.

Humility is something that we can feel. We feel it most in the attitudes and responses of others. How easy to be with the person who seldom thinks of himself. What a delight when another person hears what you say and responds with genuine interest and love. Grace flows through the humble when they place us at the center of the conversation. Do these demonstrations of humility reveal a transformed character, and not merely pious practices?

20. The Realization of Nothingness

What does it mean to become nothing when you have made me in your image? How can I eradicate the self that you have made? Yet, Merton says, "Our meditation should begin with the realization of our nothingness and helplessness in the presence of God."

The "nothing" of which the contemplative speaks does not mean non-being; how can we cease being part of God's eternal intention? Making us "nothing" in the sense of making us disappear would reverse the divine intention for all who seek the face of God. When we come before God, we recognize the "nothingness" of our power to create our self or to sustain our self. If God does not breathe in us, we have no breath at all.

Suppose that we heard these words from God: "Begin your contemplation with a sense of the 'nothingness' of your efforts and good works and noble intentions. These are most noble and pleasing to me but when you begin your prayer with your own accomplishments, you are attending to you rather than me. When you lay these aside, you come to me with 'nothing' and 'nothing' creates no separation between us.

"Your prayer begins with your nothingness because as a creature you have no power to ascend into my presence; you have no basis to make demands. Besides, when you approach me with prayer and worship techniques, these become 'something' and actually create barriers. All the words my lovers have written about their contemplation of me eventually become useless because you are not on their journey, but yours. Learn, therefore, to be on your own journey.

"To have no images or expectations in your prayer is another form of 'nothingness' that aids your prayer. If you impose your image upon your intercourse with me, your prayer becomes an idol, that is, the image and the anticipation become idols. Come to me with no expectations and you will never be disappointed. Your prayer will be what it is. I will fill the nothingness of your spiritual power. Your prayer will be the 'something' that I make it: the nothingness of your efforts, the nothingness of methods and models, and the nothingness of expectations. Only in this state of nothingness can I unite with you."

21. Return to the Center

Sometimes Merton baffles me with his radical claims: "One reason why our meditation never gets started is perhaps that we never make this real serious return to the center of our own nothingness before God."

I asked God, "What is the center of nothingness?"

The center of nothingness, my child, exists in you. It is that center point where the silence directs you; it is the anteroom to both the abyss and the holy; it is that spiritual arena where you meet me and find your deepest relation with me. This Center of your own being is not the center of nothingness but it contains your nothingness.

To begin your meditation, embrace the silence and permit it to draw you to the Center. At the Center recognize the nothingness of all that would commend you—every form, every method and every technique of prayer—and turn toward me with no expectations. Artificial expectations will on the one hand cause you to claim experiences that are not true and on the other they will blind you to the actual presence at work in you.

Another form of resistance that keeps you from the Center of nothingness lurks in the image of the Self. Your mind will go to great lengths to resist the dissolution of the false ego. This form of self has been shaped by your efforts to create an identity that wards off the chaos of your creative depth. You must also recognize this false ego as a shield against the abyss. Let go piece by piece of this false self and as it dissolves you will feel yourself sinking into the Center of your own nothingness.

You will discover that standing naked in the center of your nothingness permits the Light to shine in you. In this Light you will see light. It will lead you fearlessly through the darkness of the abyss and bring you into the Kingdom of Light. This intimacy with me can only occur when you pray from the Center of your nothingness.

22. Moment by Moment Renewal

God makes each successive, unfolding moment a Grace event. In each moment the manifestation of the Infinite Mystery appears before us and within us through God's all embracing love. In this moment, this very instant, the Grace of God inhabits the center of what is happening to you. Grace engages the moment and whatever else appears in this moment, whether regret or guilt or fear. Everything in the moment engages this unconquerable Grace. The grace that comes as the center of every moment also pervasively saturates all things with mercy.

Guilt met me in a confrontational moment when I felt accused. Old guilty feelings began to flood my mind. For once instead of taking the downhill road always filled with grief and low self-esteem, Grace came to me and I embraced it. In that moment when my self-image received a slash, I looked hard at my sin and Grace prevailed. It will always be this way, whatever the moment brings; Grace resides at the center of that moment.

God's love, which is so great, if apprehended in large doses, chokes and paralyzes us. So it comes in small pieces, little flakes that offer sufficient strength or courage or healing for that one moment. "Moment by moment I'm kept by his love, moment by moment I've life from above," so says the old hymn.

This bite-sized energy and mercy never run out. The Eternal One keeps coming and this divine initiative constantly renews Grace. As eager journeyers we must seek always to remember that God's presence as Grace comes wrapped in every moment, and from time to time we can recognize the very instant as a God-infused moment.

All this is true because God, personally and directly, renews and continuously distributes divine Grace in the moment. And this ever-present Grace invites contemplation.

23. Unitive Knowledge

At first the idea of unitive knowledge of God is so astounding that the soul can only shiver in awe. It suggests a relationship that staggers reason. What does unitive mean? Is it the unity of fresh water flowing into the sea and eventually becoming salty? Or, is it the flowing of a backwater tributary into the Amazon without the distinction completely blurring where the rivers meet? Even in the deepest unity with the divine do not human elements remain? Does not the incarnation of the Word inversely suggest that the divine does not lose its divinity in becoming human? In a similar fashion the human retains the attributes of humanness in a unitive knowledge of the divine.

For persons shaped in the Reformed tradition, unitive knowledge suggests too much intimacy with the holy. Yet according to Merton and others on the contemplative path, this knowledge of God is not only possible, but also the divine intention. Merton says, "The unitive knowledge of God in love is not knowledge of an object by a subject... but a transcendent kind of knowledge in which the created self ... seems to disappear in God and to know him alone."

Marriage offers another image of unitive knowledge that does not destroy individuality. The ecstasy of sexual intercourse climaxes in the momentary loss of individuality and it lingers with a transforming effect on both partners. To know in marriage means that two become one, even become one flesh. Yet in the metaphorical use of "becoming one flesh," both men and women retain their own bodies. Paradoxically, unitive knowledge makes two one and yet they remain two; God and humans become one, but they remain divine and human simultaneously.

So unitive knowledge in these instances does not mean the loss of personhood or individual identity. For this reason in a marriage ceremony when two candles light the third, the original two are not extinguished.

Merton seems to suggest the created Self, the Original Self of God's intention, does momentarily, but only momentarily, lose all awareness of its distinctiveness. But like the sexual climax in marital union, when the ecstasy fades, the individual remains, yet changed.

24. As Real As I

Merton asks, "What is this other level (of knowing)? It is a level of immediate intuition in an experience that impresses itself upon us directly without ambiguity – a level on which we experience reality as we experience our own being. One does not have to prove he exists, he knows it."

Each moment offers the amazing possibility of knowing God experientially, and with the certitude that I know I exist. Unitive knowledge is as real as I am; it is not an illusion. Such a possibility offers the chance of a lifetime, an invitation that no sane person could resist despite the testing and trial and darkness. No price is too great or test too severe to detract the serious person from this path.

Descartes' certitude has dominated western thought for generations: "I think, therefore I am." Experiential knowing reverses Descartes' principle by leading us to cease thinking and directs us to intuit Reality directly. We intuit Reality with the same certainty that we intuit our own existence. Indeed this Reality is part of me; it is my eternal ground and the ground of all things.

For years we may have felt the attraction of this inner way. Perhaps we have prayed our way through various stages of spiritual awareness. Something seems to lie ahead of us. Increasingly we are drawn into the contemplative way. As we walk this way, one day the Reality bursts upon us with transforming energy. Or, the awareness of this profound Reality may gradually engulf us. To each person God comes in exactly the manner that one needs and is capable of receiving the Presence.

25. Doubting God

The way to intuitive knowing passes through darkness, the desert, and the way of "unknowing." The darkness of contemplation erases all the images of God, all feeling of the divine presence, and neutralizes our ability to think God. In the sightless darkness of the abyss no hand reaches out to touch us, no Voice speaks, and no vision comes before our eyes. All that has been familiar disappears; we are left with God whom we cannot name.

In the darkness of the abyss doubts about God eat away at the soul. The gnawing pain of doubt occurs in contemplative darkness where we not only question God's existence, but we question the value of resting in stillness among the shadows. After decades of trusting God, all that we have previously depended upon for direction and certitude has vanished.

No wonder that so few walk the road into the center of this darkness. What sacrifice it requires! All our lives we have worked feverishly to acquire an understanding of God inspired by scripture and tradition, one that makes sense in the light of our experience of life. Though this derived image of God may have served us well, now it also must fall into the abyss and be consumed. Without images we are like naked people standing in darkness groping our way in faith.

In the Center of the abyss of nothingness our helplessness appears in its most desperate form. Not only does the soul lose its known modes of contact with God, but it also gives up all efforts to grasp the Infinite. In our total impotency the perceived reality of God recedes and we feel

161

alone. But in our aloneness and emptiness a presence apprehends us with a certitude of which we cannot speak. The dividing line between absolute faith and total unfaith is fine indeed.

26. Without Images

In the adolescence of faith I endeavored to read *The Dark Night of the Soul* but the words made no sense to me, so I never finished reading it. I also read *The Cloud of Unknowing* with no greater appreciation. These two books were mapping a region over which I was not traveling; the authors indicated tunnels and dangerous territory that I had never passed through. Two decades ago I again read *The Cloud*, one page each day or at the most two. The words on the page began to evoke images in my mind and touched my shallow experiences of contemplation.

As I read *The Cloud* and *The Ascent to Mount Carmel*, I distinctly heard the writers stating that the existential pathway to God leads through deep darkness. It became lucidly clear to me that in the cloud of darkness I would lose all feelings, all reason, and all images of the Holy, Sacred Mystery. After years of collecting dust on the shelf, these books were now describing clearly the spiritual landscape over which I was passing and the territory which yet lay before me.

At that moment I did not desire "the Darkness" or "the Cloud." I resisted thinking about the darkness of faith, even fearing the thought when it seeped into my consciousness. For two decades the pathway of contemplation has stretched out before me as the way not chosen. I was like a driver circling a city regularly passing up thoroughfares that would lead to the city's center.

Today I have a choice of taking the contemplative pathway to the center, but in a sense the choice seems to have been made for me. All other ways are closing for me except this one way. This path leads into the night where there are no images, no visions, and few consolations. In this setting the Divine Mystery engulfs me but in ways that the invisible presence cannot be named, nurtured or owned. Perhaps I am "entering the night in which God is present without any image, invisible, inscrutable, and beyond any satisfactory representation."

I feel that I am on a path that I did not choose to walk but if I am to be apprehended by the God beyond all names and images, I must follow one step at a time. I am afraid. I am lost. I cannot go through this night in my strength alone. I must be taken like a blind child in an unfamiliar house and led from room to room. Mingled with my fear I find a tiny bit of confidence that for "the joy set before me," I will enter the darkness. I will be led by a soundless Voice, held by an invisible Hand and understood by inscrutable Wisdom.

27. Incommunicado Contemplative

The way of unknowing is often the way of unspeaking. When we 'see' without seeing, 'hear' without sounds, 'smell' without a scent, and 'taste' without chewing, little wonder words fail us. How can a language born of sense describe the experience born of spirit, especially the Infinite Spirit?

With searching spirits we reflect on the 'manifest mystery' in Jesus. His life, teaching and ministry open the door to meditation, but the 'unmanifest mystery,' which the contemplative explores, has no such referent. Thus, our exposure to this unmanifest holiness leaves us without a means either to reflect on the experience or to describe with words because the event resists all the attempts of human language. All imaginative efforts also fail because that for which we search lies outside the range of our capacities.

So when we walk through the looking glass and the 'Infinite Mystery' engages us, what can we say about it? On this pathway of unknowing we are met by One we cannot name, experience what we cannot explain, and are transformed without being able to recount it.

No wonder this way borders on a-theism. We cannot even conceive this reality, so how can we speak of it to another. No logic can persuade us of the Divine Mystery. Yet, though we do not know God in a conventional manner, our souls rest in an unshakable certainty. It is a certitude expressed in a passion for God and a peace that emanates from the Mystery; this conviction gives us the courage to stay the course when we have no idea where it is leading.

Is it strange that I write so much about what cannot be put into words?

28. Enlightened Eyes

When our prayer leads us to the Palace of Nowhere, we see "everywhere" in a very different light. In this palace all the lines of sight converge, and the tall, clear windows give a God-hue to everything. The windows provide a reflection into which we look and see everything in the Light of God -- the image of the world, the reality of all persons and the story of the human race.

A life lived in darkness bursts into the Light and in God's Light we see Light. The way of unknowing and the imageless unseeing lead to a place of pure knowing and clear vision. Without the hand that guides us, and the light that gives us vision, we would be void of direction. Mystery, O Mystery; Paradox, O Paradox!

Amazingly, when we see the world in the light of God, a dim pattern begins to emerge, and through a glass darkly we see the themes of the human story that have been and still are being played out on the planetary landscape. And bits and pieces of that pattern now and then begin to appear in our own unfolding story. When we notice this pattern forming, our suspicion that Someone is directing our lives receives validation.

From this Palace of Nowhere in which all things converge and the Light lights all in the world and will light all coming into the world, both the direction of our lives and the importance of the things that we are to do draw us into the world. In order to return to our senses, we must be led by the Light into the world with seeing eyes and yearning hearts.

29. Without Understanding

I realize that my journey is now leading me into a mystery that I do not understand. Perhaps in the concreteness of the present moment I am experiencing a manifestation of the unmanifest mystery of God. In the darkness through which I am passing I have none of the familiar signposts that previously gave me my bearings. In the deep silences of rest stops along the way the Voice does not speak often.

In this incomprehensibly dark mystery I am aware of being wrapped in a Presence that enables me to move forward. Often when I am not anticipating a word of any kind, the Voice speaks. Today it was a short phrase from Eugene Peterson's paraphrase of a passage in I Peter: "God takes delight in just plain people."

Throughout my life I have claimed to be ordinary and plain. And I think God picked out this phrase to assure me that not only am I being led, but also I am a delight.

The journey into contemplation promises a Presence that on occasion becomes manifest to me. And, the Presence bears a meaning but I cannot express it, yet it is with me and in me.

All these events that I am struggling to describe confirm my new Venue. Without my asking for it consciously or even desiring it, the God of Mystery guides me into a dimension of life I have not known or even imagined. I hesitate to admit it to myself, but this seems to be the place that I am to explore in this era of life. In my final months of teaching why did I wonder if my spirituality was simply for the sake of my work? I see so clearly now that nothing can ever satisfy my soul but God, whether I am pursuing a Christian vocation or simply living from day to day. I cannot help yearning for and submitting myself to the darkness and the silence. At last, I think I am beginning to understand the "darkness of faith" that brother Carlo wrote about. For many years I had no idea what he meant by those words.

30. God Alone

I wonder what hour it is in my life. Is it the 7th hour, each representing a decade? Or, is it much later. Does the garden await us all at the end of our days?

For a moment I had a brief flash of insight. This is the garden era; the darkness has fallen; support from all else has disappeared – work, place, role, old identity and support from all false hopes. I am left with silence; in the silence of the garden I can only offer myself to God.

God! The freedom of nothingness! Nothing to achieve, nothing to cling to, nothing to offer but a self, well worn and stripped of window dressing!

There is a spot in the garden with a homelike feeling. As I pray in this garden I want to find hope. This garden lies near the end of my journey as it did for my Savior. He knew the despair of rejection, the abusive anger of those in authority and the human flinching at the edge of the abyss. Yet, in the darkness of the hour he could relinquish his will to the Larger Will at work. Hope empowered Him to face into the mystery.

And, there is something else in the garden – the raw encounter with

165

the Mystery. "The hour of hope: God alone." I cannot speak here of knowing God but of meeting, being embraced and being taken into the Divine Mystery of Love – the Trinitarian community of Love. Perhaps washed, bathed, embraced, filled and transformed provide metaphors for apprehending the dark side of the mystery. When all images dissolve, when all metaphors fade, I experience God as faceless, unknown, unfelt, but undeniably God.

Indubitably God – Yes!

31. Old Helps In Prayer

Contemplation may or may not be a higher form of prayer. It seems presumptuous to label one spiritual passion or pathway as higher or greater than another. A discussion of the darkness of the mystery and the prayer of unknowing and the certitude of the heart and not of the mind seems so out of reach for the ordinary Christian. Too long these descriptions and terms seemed to place the contemplative life beyond the reach of ordinary believers.

By noting these difficulties we are not arguing against contemplation as a way into a more passionate relationship with God, but we should not forget that many saints have had nothing to say of contemplation as we have described it. In utter sincerity and simplicity they offered praise, spoke thanksgiving, made confession and prayed for family and friends and the needs of the world. They knew God! Who is to deny that they knew God in ways untouched by contemplation as we have discussed it? Like all obedient disciples of Jesus, they followed the path on which their feet had been placed. Perhaps in their faithful, loving practice, they were united with God by seamless stitching that the mystics and contemplatives have longed for.

Other followers of Jesus became contemplatives because word-prayers dried up and ceased to express their hearts' desires. Mental prayers also lost their grip on their hearts, and the imagination ceased to draw life from the scriptures or from nature or mysterious providence they experienced in daily living. All these proven ways seem to fade in their usefulness to mediate God

At some point a doorway opened and the Spirit drew them into silence, brushed them with the mystery and kept them on a path that led into and through the thick darkness. In moments of revelation they knew what it meant to be grasped by God – apprehended by that which they had not comprehended.

Still from time to time these veterans of the 'dark night' again uttered God's praise and with their lips gave thanks and confessed their sin. So the contemplative often steps out of the world of abstraction, vagueness and the mysterious realm of incommunicable experience into the world where "Thank you, Father" is also deep and genuine prayer.

32. Core of Religious Life

The fervor and vitality of the life of God in us and in the Church dries up unless it is replenished through contemplation. This simple statement seems axiomatic, so obvious that it appears redundant. Yet, many of the Church's leaders are completely unaware of this inner way of knowing. This assessment may border on judgment and show a lack of compassionate understanding. Nevertheless, if spiritual and ecclesiastical leaders do not talk about a personal knowledge of God, practice the art of self-giving love, and give evidence of having passed through their own darkness into the Light of God, how can they become commentators on this pathway? Consequently, their words stick to their tongues or tumble lifelessly into the air because they lack the life-giving spirit.

Christian faith today, as always, depends upon a personal relationship with God. Those who have set aside this personal dimension by submission to the rationalism of the age seem never to consider that the experience of God is essential to faith and faithfulness. Not only the skeptic loses out but persons frozen in a rigid belief structure also pay little attention to conscious contact with God. Everything is already settled for them and they need only to repeat the old words and phrases to reassure themselves. How long can persons live by the perceptions of others who looked through eyes conditioned by a very different environment? To the skeptics and fundamentalists we add the persons who once had dealings with God but have ceased seeking and seemingly have lost their sensitivity to the Spirit. For these reasons, the deep truth of God in Christ and Christ in us withers away. The "form of religion" remains but the power has drained out.

The consistency of life and the supernatural power of the Spirit, I am convinced, can be created in all of us; it can be renewed in us if it has faded; and the fervor born in the contemplation of God would be life-giving to millions today. For every 'would be' spiritual person a path to contemplation lies just beneath the next step.

What enormous value would be derived from an honest assessment of life! Who are you? What is going on in your life? What are your needs, hungers and desires?

The "way" that lies immediately before you leads straight from your heart. Out of the stillness comes a hunger, a desire for 'Something' and the something is a "Someone," God. When given attention and heeded seriously, the desire will find the pathway and a hand you do not see, on a way you do not know will lead you to an end you do not choose.

33. The Transformation of Life

Contemplation leads to the transformation of life. We cannot enter deeply into God's presence and maintain an unfeeling heart. The love of God crushes our hardness and renders it dust so that it may be mingled with love and molded into a soft resilient compassion. Physically exercising the muscles like the biceps and triceps makes a fit and strong body, but overworking the heart causes it to harden into inefficiency.

The emptiness of contemplation leads to clarity of thought and simplicity of focus. These twin gifts engage the mind as deeply as the heart. With this clarity of thought, the grossness of lust and prejudice and retribution find no place. The old habits of the heart do not fade rapidly or easily, but they cannot endure the light of Love.

Humility, the fruit of long and studied contemplation, exposes arrogance as a false self. The arrogance at the core of the soul consists of the refusal to be our true Self, and it reveals an ambiguous and empty effort to create an idealized but illusory self.

If our contemplation matures, it will be because our wills have ceased to resist God's will and we have begun to embrace the simple reality of who we are and the importance of our place in the world. So contemplation, far from causing us to turn from the world in a cowardly escapism or the subtle denial of material reality, leads us straight into life with eyes wide-open to God. And we begin to see God, even if momentarily, in the concreteness of the present moment. We think it fair to say that the person who meditates participates in the sacred reality of each moment in a manner that the detached observer cannot.

Epilogue

Could God be speaking these words to you today?

"My friend, I do love you and I will keep saying my love to you until you believe that it is I and not you, my voice and not your unconscious longing. Now is the time for you to relinquish your fear and doubt. Plunge into me, into my love for you and live in my freedom.

"True, it is this moment in which I come to you and this fresh moment is a new creation, a new beginning for you. It is always NEW moment after moment. In every new moment I am present – not in things but in time. I am there to awaken you and guide you toward the fulfillment of your life and my purpose, which are one.

"What is the Moment? I am in the moment, the world inside you and outside you is all in the moment, all the possibilities for the future reside in this moment. All is well in this moment! It is as it is – and this is where you need a healthy eye to see this moment as it is. It is a moment of light – it will illuminate your life – it radiates the light that overcomes the darkness. It eliminates the competition of other gods."

Contemplative Bibliography

Anonymous. *The Cloud of Unknowing*. Garden City, New York: Doubleday (Image Books), 1973

Bourgeault, Cynthia. *Centering Prayer and Inner Awakening*. Cambridge, Massachusetts: Cowley Publications, 2004.

Carretto, Carlo. *Letters from the Desert*. Maryknoll, New York: Orbis Books, 1972.

De Caussade, Jean-Pierre. *Abandonment to Divine Providence*. Garden City, New York: Image Books, 1975

Evans, Gene. *Practicing His Presence*. (Frank Laubach and Brother Lawrence) Goleta, California: Christian Books, 1973

Finley, James. *The Contemplative Heart*. Notre Dame, Indiana: Sorin Books, 2000.

Jager, Willigis. *The Way to Contemplation: Encountering God Today*. New York: Paulist Press, 1987.

Keating, Thomas. *Open Mind, Open Heart, The Contemplative Dimension of the Gospel*. New York: Continuum, 1994.

Kelly, Thomas. *A Testament of Devotion*. San Francisco: Harper & Row, 1941.

Merton, Thomas. *New Seeds of Contemplation*. New York, New York: New Directions Publishing Corporation, 1961

_____ *Contemplative Prayer*. New York: Doubleday (Image Books), 1996.

_____ *The Inner Experience: Notes on Contemplation*. San Francisco: Harper Collins Publishers, 2003.

Pennington, M. Basil. *Centering Prayer: Renewing an Ancient Christian Prayer Form*. New York: Image Books (Doubleday), 1980.